On

Also by J. Krishnamurti

The Awakening of Intelligence
Education and the Significance of Life
The Ending of Time (with David Bohm)
Exploration into Insight
The First and Last Freedom
The Flame of Attention
Freedom from the Known
The Future of Humanity (with David Bohm)
Krishnamurti to Himself
Krishnamurti's Notebook
Life Ahead
The Network of Thought
On Fear
On Freedom
On God
On Living and Dying
On Love and Loneliness
On Mind and Thought
On Nature and the Environment
On Relationship
On Right Livelihood
Truth and Actuality
The Wholeness of Life

On Truth

J. Krishnamurti

EastWest Books (Madras) Pvt. Ltd.,
• Chennai • Bangalore • Hyderabad • New Delhi

EastWest Books (Madras) Pvt. Ltd.,
571, Poonamalle High Road, Aminjikarai, Chennai - 600 029.
E-mail : ewb@touchtelindia.net
3-5-1108, Maruti Complex, II Floor, Narayanaguda, Hyderabad - 500 029.
53/2, Bull Temple Road, Basavangudi, Bangalore - 560 019.
A-10, Lower Ground Floor, Lajpat Nagar III, New Delhi - 110 024.

ON TRUTH Copyright © 1995 by
Krishnamurti Foundation Trust Ltd and Krishnamurti Foundation of America

Series editor: Mary Cadogan
Associate editors: Ray McCoy and David Skitt

First EastWest Books paperback edition 2004

All rights reserved. No part of this publication may be used or reproduced, stored in a retrieval system, or transmitted, in any form or by any means, electronic, mechanical, photocopying, recording or otherwise, without the prior written permission of the publisher.

For additional information about Krishnamurti Schools, Centres and other publications contact:
Krishnamurti Foundation Trust Ltd
Brockwood Park, Bramdean, Hampshire, SO24 0LQ, England
E-mail: info@brockwood.org.uk Website: www.kfoundation.org
or
Krishnamurti Foundation of America
P.O. Box 1560, Ojai, California 93024-1560, U.S.A.
E-mail: kfa@kfa.org Website: www.kfa.org
or
Krishnamurti Foundation India
Vasanta Vihar, 124/126 Greenways Road, RA Puram, Chennai - 600 028, India
E-mail: kfihq@md2.vsnl.net.in Website: www.kfionline.org

ISBN : 81-88661-23-6

Cover design J. Menon

Printed at Sri Venkatesa Printing House, Chennai 600 026
E.mail: saicure@vsnl.com

Religion means exploring with doubt, questioning sceptically, investigating what is truth. That is religion.

Ojai, 2 May 1981

Contents

ix	Foreword
1	Poona, 3 October 1948
10	Rajghat, 23 January 1949
16	Rajahmundry, 20 November 1949
20	Bombay, 12 March 1950
24	London, 23 April 1952
34	Talk to Students at Rajghat, 31 December 1952
36	Bombay, 8 February 1953
38	Poona, 10 September 1958
51	From *Truth and Actuality*, Brockwood Park, 18 May 1975
64	Saanen, 1 August 1975
73	From *Truth and Actuality*, Saanen, 25 July 1976
75	Conversation at Brockwood Park, 28 June 1979
111	Ojai, California, 8 May 1980
114	Bombay, 3 February 1985
120	Bombay, 7 February 1985
122	Bombay, 9 February 1985
129	From *Last Talks at Saanen 1985*, 21 July 1985
131	From *Last Talks at Saanen 1985*, 25 July 1985
134	Brockwood Park, 29 August 1985
143	Sources and Acknowledgments

Foreword

JIDDU KRISHNAMURTI WAS born in India in 1895 and, at the age of thirteen, was taken up by the Theosophical Society, which considered him to be the vehicle for the 'world teacher' whose advent it had been proclaiming. Krishnamurti was soon to emerge as a powerful, uncompromising, and unclassifiable teacher, whose talks and writings were not linked to any specific religion and were neither of the East nor the West but for the whole world. Firmly repudiating the messianic image, in 1929 he dramatically dissolved the large and monied organization that had been built around him and declared truth to be 'a pathless land', which could not be approached by any formalized religion, philosophy, or sect.

For the rest of his life Krishnamurti insistently rejected the guru status that others tried to foist upon him. He continued to attract large audiences throughout the world but claimed no authority, wanted no disciples, and spoke always as one individual to another. At the core of his teaching was the realization that fundamental changes in society can be brought about only by a transformation of individual consciousness. The need for self-knowledge and understanding of the restrictive, separative influences of religious and nationalistic conditionings was constantly stressed. Krishnamurti pointed always to the urgent need for openness, for that "vast space in the brain in which there is unimaginable energy." This seems to have been the wellspring of his own creativity and the key to his catalytic impact on such a wide variety of people.

Krishnamurti continued to speak all over the world until he died in 1986 at the age of ninety. His talks and dialogues, journals and letters have been preserved in over sixty books and hundreds of recordings. From that vast body of teachings this series of theme books has been compiled. Each book focuses on an issue that has particular relevance to and urgency in our daily lives.

Poona, 3 October 1948

Questioner: Memory, you say, is incomplete experience. I have a memory and a vivid impression of your previous talks. In what sense is this an incomplete experience? Please explain this in detail.

Krishnamurti: What do we mean by memory? You go to school, and are full of facts, technical knowledge. If you are an engineer, you use the memory of technical knowledge to build a bridge. That is factual memory. There is also psychological memory. You have said something to me, pleasant or unpleasant, and I retain it; and when I next meet you, I meet you with that memory, the memory of what you have said or have not said.

So there are two facets to memory, the psychological and the factual. They are always interrelated, and therefore not clearcut. We know that factual memory is essential as a means of livelihood. But is psychological memory essential? And what is the factor that retains the psychological memory? What makes one remember insult or praise? Why does one retain some memories and reject others? Obviously, one retains memories that are pleasant, and avoids those that are unpleasant. If you observe, you will see that painful memories are put aside quicker than pleasurable ones. And mind is memory, at whatever level, by whatever name you call it; mind is the product of the past, it is founded on the past, which is memory, a conditioned state.

Now, with that memory we meet life, we meet a new challenge. The challenge is always new, and our response is always old, because it is the outcome of the past. So experiencing without memory is one state, and experiencing with memory is another. That is, there is a challenge, which is always new. I meet it with the response, with the condition of the old. So what happens? I absorb the new, I do not understand it; and the experiencing of the new is conditioned by the past. Therefore, there is a partial understanding of the new, there is never complete understanding. It is only when there is complete understanding of anything that it does not leave the scar of memory.

When there is a challenge, which is ever new, you meet it with the response of the old. The old response conditions the new, and therefore twists it, gives it a bias. There is therefore no complete understanding of the new; hence the new is absorbed into the old, and thereby strengthens the old. This may seem abstract, but it is not difficult if you go into it a little closely and carefully. The situation in the world at the present time demands a new approach, a new way of tackling the world problem, which is ever new. We are incapable of approaching it because we approach it with our conditioned minds, with national, local, family, and religious prejudices. That is, our previous experiences are acting as a barrier to the understanding of the new challenge, so we go on cultivating and strengthening memory and, therefore, never understand the new; we never meet the challenge completely. It is only when one is able to meet the challenge anew, afresh, without the past, that it yields its fruits, its riches.

The questioner says, 'I have a memory and a vivid impression of your previous talks. In what sense is this an incomplete experience?' Obviously, it is an incomplete experience if it is merely an impression, a memory. If you understand what has been said, see the truth of it, that truth is not a memory. Truth is not a memory, because truth is ever new, constantly transforming itself. You have a memory of the previous talk. Why? Because you are using the previous talk as a guide, you have not fully understood it. You want to go into it, and unconsciously or consciously it is being maintained. But if you understand something completely, that is, see the truth of something wholly, you will find there is no memory whatsoever.

Our education is the cultivation of memory, the strengthening of memory. Your religious practices and rituals, your reading and knowledge, are all the strengthening of memory. What do we mean by that? Why do we hold to memory? I do not know if you have noticed that, as you grow older, you look to the past, to its joys, its pains, its pleasures; and if one is young, one looks to the future. Why are we doing this? Why has memory become so important? For the simple and obvious reason that we do not know how to live wholly, completely in the present. We are using the present as a means to the future, and therefore the present has no significance. We cannot live in the present because we are using the present as a passage to the future. Because I am going to become something, there is never a complete understanding of myself, and understanding myself—what I am exactly now—does not require the cultivation of memory. On the contrary, memory is a hindrance to the understanding of what is.

I do not know if you have noticed that a new thought, a new feeling, comes only when the mind is not caught in the net of memory. There is an interval between two thoughts, between two memories, and when that interval can be maintained, then out of that interval comes a new state of being that is no longer memory. We have memories, and we cultivate memory, as a means of continuance. That is, the 'me' and the 'mine' become very important as long as the cultivation of memory exists; and as most of us are made up of 'me' and 'mine', memory plays a very important part in our lives. If you had no memory, your property, your family, your ideas, would not be important as such; so to give strength to 'me' and 'mine', you cultivate memory. But if you observe, you will see that there is an interval between two thoughts, between two emotions. In that interval, which is not the product of memory, there is an extraordinary freedom from the 'me' and the 'mine', and that interval is timeless.

Let us look at the problem differently. Surely, memory is time, is it not? That is, memory creates yesterday, today, and tomorrow. Memory of yesterday conditions today and therefore shapes tomorrow. That is, the past through the present creates the future. There is a time process going on, which is the will to become. Memory is time, and through time we hope to achieve a result. I am a clerk today and, given time and opportunity, I will become the manager or the owner. So I must have time; and with the same mentality we say, 'I shall achieve reality, I shall approach God'. Therefore, I must have time to realize, which means I must cultivate memory, strengthen memory by practice, by discipline, to be something, to achieve, to gain, which means continuation in time. So through time we hope to achieve the timeless, through time we hope to gain the eternal. Can you do that? Can you catch the eternal in the net of time, through memory, which is of time?

The timeless can be only when memory, which is the 'me' and the 'mine', ceases. If you see the truth of that—that through time the timeless cannot be understood or received—then we go into the problem of memory. The memory of technical things is essential; but the psychological memory that maintains the self, the 'me' and the 'mine', that gives identification and self-continuance, is wholly detrimental to life and to reality. When one sees the truth of that, the false drops away; therefore, there is no psychological retention of yesterday's experience.

You see a lovely sunset, a beautiful tree in a field, and when you first look at it, you enjoy it completely, wholly; but then you go back to it with the desire to enjoy it again. What happens when you do that? There is no enjoyment, because it is the memory of yesterday's sunset that is now making you return, that is pushing, urging you to enjoy. Yesterday there was no memory, only a spontaneous appreciation, a direct response; but today you are desirous of recapturing the experience of yesterday. That is, memory is intervening between you and the sunset; therefore, there is no enjoyment, no richness, no fullness of beauty. Again, you have a friend who said something to you yesterday, an insult or a compliment, and you retain that memory; and with that memory you meet your friend today. You do not really meet your friend—you carry with you the memory of yesterday, which intervenes; and so we go on, surrounding ourselves and our actions with memory, and therefore there is no newness, no freshness. That is why memory makes life weary, dull, and empty.

We live in antagonism with one another because the 'me' and the 'mine' are strengthened through memory. Memory comes to life through action in the present; we give life to memory through the present, but when we do not give life to memory, it fades away. So memory of facts, of technical things, is an obvious necessity, but memory as psychological retention is detrimental to the understanding of life, to communion with one another.

Q: You have said that when the conscious mind is still, the subconscions projects itself. Is the subconscious a superior entity? Is it not necessary to pour out all that is hidden in the labyrinths of the subconscious in order to decondition oneself? How can one go about it?

K: I wonder how many of us are aware that there is a subconscious, and that there are different layers in our consciousness? I think most of us are aware only of the superficial mind, of the daily activities, of the rattling, superficial consciousness. We are not aware of the depth, the significance and meaning of the hidden layers; and occasionally, through a dream, through a hint, through an intimation, one is aware that there are other states of being. Most of us are too busy, too occupied with our lives, with amusements, with lustful desires, with our vanities, to be aware of anything but the superficial. Most of us spend our lives in the struggle for power, political or personal, for position, for achievement.

Now the questioner asks, 'Is the subconscious a superior entity?' That is the first point. Is there a superior entity apart from the thought process? Surely, as long as the thought process exists, though it may divide itself up into inferior and superior, there can be no superior entity, no permanent entity apart from that which is transitory. So we will have to look into this question very carefully and understand the whole significance of consciousness. I have said that when you have a problem and have thought about it until your mind is weary without finding the answer, it often happens that when you sleep on it the answer is found by morning. While the conscious mind is still, the hidden layers of the unconscious mind are at work on the problem, and when you wake up you find the answer. Surely that means that the hidden layers of the mind do not sleep when you go to sleep, but are working all the time.

Though the conscious mind may be asleep, the unconscious, in its different layers, is grappling with that problem, and naturally it projects itself onto the conscious. Now the question is, is that a superior entity? Obviously not. What do you mean by *superior entity?* You mean, do you not, a spiritual entity, an entity that is beyond time? You are full of thoughts, and an entity that you can think about is surely not a spiritual entity—it is part of thought; therefore, it is a child of thought, still within the field of thought. Call it what you will, it is still a product of thought; therefore, it is a product of time, and not a spiritual entity.

The next question is, 'Is it not necessary to pour out all that is hidden in the labyrinths of the subconscious in order to decondition oneself? How can one go about it?' As I said, consciousness has different layers. First, there is the superficial layer, and below that there is memory, because without memory there is no action. Underneath that there is the desire to be, to become, the desire to fulfil. If you go still deeper, you will find a state of complete negation, of uncertainty, of void. This whole totality is consciousness. Now, as long as there is the desire to be, to become, to achieve, to gain, there must be the strengthening of the many layers of consciousness as the 'me' and the 'mine', and the emptying of those many layers can come about only when one understands the process of becoming. That is, as long as there is the desire to be, to become, to achieve, memory is strengthened, and from that memory there is action, which only further conditions the mind. I hope you are interested in all this. If not, it does not matter; but I will go on, because some of you may be aware of this problem.

Life is not just one layer of consciousness, it is not just one leaf, one branch: life is a whole, total process. We must understand the total process before we can understand the beauty of life, its greatness, its pains, its sorrows and its joys. Now, to empty the subconscious, which is to understand the whole state of being, of consciousness, we must see what it is made up of; we must be aware of the various forms of conditioning that are the memories of race, family, group, and so on, the various experiences that are not complete. Now, one can analyze these memories, take each response, each memory, and unravel it, go into it fully and dissolve it; but for that one would need infinite time, patience, and care. Surely there must be a different approach to the problem.

Anyone who has thought about it at all is familiar with the process of taking up a response, analyzing it, following it, and dissolving it, and doing that with every response; and if one does not analyse a response fully, or misses something in that analysis, then one goes back and spends long days in this unfruitful process. There must be a different approach to deconditioning the whole being of memories, so that the mind may be new every moment. How is it to be done? Do you understand the problem? It is this: We are used to meeting life with old memories, old traditions, old habits; we meet today with yesterday. Now, can one meet today, the present, without the thought of yesterday? Surely, that is a new question, is it not? We know the old method of going step-by-step, analysing each response, dissolving it through practice, discipline, and so on. We see that such a method involves time; and when you use time as a means of deconditioning, obviously it only strengthens the condition. If I use time as a means of freeing myself, in that very process I am becoming conditioned.

So what am I to do? Since it is a new question, I must approach it anew. That is, can one be free immediately, instantaneously? Can there be regeneration without the element of time, which is but memory? I say that regeneration, transformation, is now, not tomorrow, and that transformation can come only when there is complete freedom from yesterday. How is one to be free from yesterday? Now, when I put that question, what is happening to your mind? What is happening to your mind when you see that your mind must be new, that your yesterday must go? When you see the truth of this, what is the state of your mind? If you want to understand a modern painting, you must obviously not approach it with your classical training. If you recognize that as a fact, what happens to your classical training? Your classical training is absent when there is the intention to understand a modern painting—the challenge is new, and you recognize that you cannot understand it through the screen of yesterday. When you see the truth of that, then yesterday is gone, there is complete purgation of yesterday.

You must see the truth that yesterday cannot translate the present. It is only truth that deconditions completely, and to see the truth of what is requires an enormous attention. Since there is no complete attention as long as there is distraction, what do we mean by distraction? When there are several interests from among which you choose one and fix your mind on it, then any interest that takes your mind away from that central interest you call distraction. Now, can you choose an interest and concentrate on that one interest? Why do you choose one interest and discard others? You choose one interest because it is more profitable; therefore, your choice is based on profit, the desire to gain; and the moment you have a desire to gain, you must resist as a distraction everything that takes your thoughts away from the central interest. Apart from your biological appetites, have you a central interest? I really question whether you have a central interest. Therefore, you are not distracted—you are merely living in a state without interest.

He who would understand the truth must give it his undivided attention, and that undivided attention comes only when there is no choice, and therefore no idea of distraction. There is no such thing as distraction, because life is a movement, and one has to understand this whole movement and not divide it into interests and distractions. One has to look therefore at everything to see the truth or falseness of it. When you see the truth of this, it liberates consciousness from yesterday. You can test it out for yourself. To see the truth about nationalism and not be caught up in the arguments pro and con, you will have to go into it and be open to all the intimations of that problem. In being aware of the problem of nationalism without condemnation or justification, in seeing the truth that it is false, you will find there comes a complete freedom from the whole issue. So it is only the perception of truth that liberates; and to see, to receive truth, there must be the focusing of attention, which means that you must give your heart and mind to see and to understand.

Rajghat, 23 January 1949

PRESUMABLY, MOST OF you have some kind of a teacher, some kind of guru, either in the Himalayas, or round the corner, some kind of guide. Now why do you need him? You do not, obviously, need him for material purposes, unless he promises you a good job the day after tomorrow. So presumably you need him for psychological purposes. Now, why? Basically, obviously, you need him because you say, 'I am confused, I do not know how to live in this world, things are too contradictory. There is confusion, there is misery, there is death, decay, degradation, disintegration; and I need somebody to advise me what to do'. Isn't that why you need a guru, why you go to a guru? You say, 'Being confused, I need a teacher who will help me to clear up the confusion, or rather help me to resolve it'. So your need is psychological. You do not treat your prime minister as your guru, because he merely deals with the material life of society. You look to him for your physical needs, whereas here you look to a teacher for your psychological needs.

Now, what do you mean by the word *need?* I need sunshine, I need food, clothes, and shelter; and in the same way, do I need a teacher? To answer that question, I must find out who has created this awful mess around me and in me. If I am responsible for the confusion, I am the only person who can clear it up, which means that I must understand it myself; but you generally go to a teacher in order that he may extricate you from the confusion, or show you the way, give you directions on how to act with regard to it. Or you say, 'Well, this world is false, I must find truth'. And the guru or the teacher says, 'I have found truth', so you go to him to partake of that truth.

Can confusion be cleared up by another, however great? Surely this confusion exists in our relationship; therefore we have to understand our relationship with one another, with society, with property, with ideas, and so on; and can someone give us the understanding of that relationship? Someone may point out, may show, but I have to understand my relationship, where I am.

Are you interested in this? My difficulty is that I feel you are not interested, because you are watching somebody else doing something. When you ask a question, do you feet the importance of listening to the answer? Isn't life important to you, something vital, creative that must be understood? You listen to be confirmed in your search for gurus, or to strengthen your own conviction that gurus are essential. That way we do not find the truth of the matter. You can find the truth of the matter by searching out your heart, why you need a guru.

Many things are involved in this question. Many seem to think that truth is static, and that therefore a guru can lead one to it. As someone can direct you to the station, so you think a guru can direct you to truth. That means truth is static; but is truth static? You would like it to be; for that which is static is very gratifying; at least you know what it is and you can hold on to it.

So you are really seeking gratification. You want security, you want the assurance of a guru, you want him to say to you: you are doing very well, carry on, you want him to give you mental comfort, an emotional pat on the back. So you go to a guru that really gratifies you, invariably. That is why there are so many gurus! And so many pupils! Which means that you are not really seeking truth: you want gratification, and the person who gives you the greatest satisfaction you call your guru. That satisfaction is either neurological, that is, physical, or psychological; and you think in his presence you feel great peace, great quietness, a sense of being understood. In other words, you want a glorified father or mother who will help you overcome the difficulty!

Have you ever sat quietly under a tree? There too you will find great peace. You will also feel that you are being understood! In other words, in the presence of a very quiet person, you also become quiet; and this quietness you attribute to the teacher. Then you put a garland around him, and kick your servant. So when you say you need a guru, surely all these things are implied in it, are they not? And the guru that assures you an escape, that guru becomes your need.

Now, confusion exists only in relationship; and why do we need someone else to help us understand this confusion? You might say now, 'What are *you* doing? Are you not acting as our guru?' I am surely not acting as your guru because, first of all, I am not giving you any gratification, I am not telling you what you should do from moment to moment or from day to day; I am just pointing something out to you; you can take it or leave it. It depends on you, not on me. I do not demand a thing from you, neither your worship, nor your flattery, nor your insults. I say this is a fact, take it or leave it. But most of you will leave it for the obvious reason that you will not find gratification in it. But the man who is really in earnest, really serious in his intention to find out, will have sufficient food in what is being said, which is that confusion exists only in your relationship, so let us therefore understand that relationship.

To understand that relationship is to be aware, not to avoid it, but to see the whole content of relationship. The truth is not in the distance, truth is near; truth is under every leaf, in every smile, in every tear, in the words, feelings, thoughts that one has. But it is so covered up that we have to uncover it to see. To uncover is to discover what is false; and the moment you know what is false, and when that drops away, the truth is there.

So truth is a thing that is living from moment to moment—to be discovered, not believed in, not quoted, not formulated. But to see that truth, your mind and your heart must be extremely pliable, alert. But most of us, unfortunately, do not want an alert, pliable, and swift mind; we want to be put to sleep by mantras, rituals. We put ourselves to sleep in so many ways! Obviously we need a certain environment, a certain atmosphere, solitude—not the pursuit or the avoidance of loneliness—but a certain aloneness, in which there is full attention; and that aloneness, that certain complete attention, is there only when you are in trouble, when your problems are really intense. And if you have a friend, if you have somebody who can help you, you go to him; but surely, to treat him as your guru is obviously immature, obviously childish. It is like seeking mother's apron strings.

When we are in difficulty, all our instinct is to turn to somebody—to the mother, to the father, of to a glorified father, whom you call a master or guru. But if the guru is worth his salt, he will tell you to understand yourself in action, which is relationship. Surely, you are far more important than the guru; you are far more important than I; because it is your life, your misery, your strife, your struggle. The guru, or I, or someone else may be free, *but what value has that for you?* The worship of the guru is detrimental to your understanding of yourself. And there is a peculiar factor in this. The more you show respect to the one, the less you show respect to others. You salute your guru profoundly and kick your subordinate. Therefore, your respect has very little significance. These are all facts. I know probably most of you do not like what has been said, because your mind wants to be comforted, it has been bruised so much. It is caught up in such trouble and misery, and it says, 'For God's sake give me some hope, some refuge'.

Only the mind that is in despair can find reality. A mind that is completely discontented can jump into reality; not a mind that is content, not a mind that is respectable, hedged by beliefs.

So you flower only in relationship; you flower only in love, not in contention. But our hearts are withered; we have filled our hearts with the things of the mind, and so we look to others to fill our minds with their creations. Since we have no love, we try to find it with the teacher, with someone else. Love is a thing that cannot be found. You cannot buy it, you cannot immolate yourself to it. Love comes into being only when the self is absent. And as long as you are seeking gratification, escapes, refusing to understand your confusion in relationship, you are merely emphasizing the self, and, therefore, denying love.

Are you being mesmerized by my voice and words? Surely, what I have said must be very disturbing to you? If it is not disturbing, something is wrong. Because one is attacking the whole structure of your thought process, your comfortable ways, and that disturbance must be very fatiguing. Let us be very clear about what we are trying to do, you and I. Probably, most of you will say, 'I know all this; Shankara, Buddha, somebody else has said this'. This statement indicates that, having read so much, superficially, you relegate what is being said to one of the pigeonholes in your mind, and thereby discard it. It is a convenient way of disposing of what you have heard, which means you are listening merely on the verbal level, and not taking in the full content, which creates a disturbance.

Peace cannot be had without a great deal of searching; and what you and I are doing is searching out our minds and hearts in order to find out what is true and what is false. And to search out is to expend energy, vitality; it should be as physically exhausting as digging! But unfortunately, many are used to listening; many are merely spectators enjoying, observing what another is playing; therefore, you are not tired. Spectators are never tired, which shows that they are not partaking in the game! You are not the spectator, and I am not the player.

You are not here to listen to a song. What you and I are trying to do is to find a song in our own hearts and not listen to the song of another. Many people are used to listening to the song of another, and so their hearts are empty, and they will always be empty because they fill their hearts with another's song. That is not your song; then you are merely gramophones, changing the record according to your mood; you are not the musicians. And especially in times of great travail and trouble, each one of us *has* to be the musician; we have to recreate ourselves with song, which means to free, to empty the heart of those things that are filled by the mind. So we have to understand the creations of the mind, and see the falseness of those creations. Then we will not fill our hearts with those creations. Then, when the heart is empty—not filled with ashes—when the heart is empty, and the mind is quiet, then there is a song, the song that cannot be destroyed or perverted, because it is not put together by the mind.

Rajahmundry, 20 November 1949

Questioner: You say that gurus are unnecessary, but how can I find truth without the wise help and guidance that only a guru can give?

Krishnamurti: The question is whether a guru is necessary or not. Can truth be found through another? Some say it can and some say it cannot. We want to know the truth of this, not my opinion against the opinion of another. I have no opinion in this matter. Either it is so or it is not. Whether it is essential that you should or should not have a guru is not a question of opinion, however profound, erudite, popular, or universal. The truth of the matter is to be found in fact.

First of all, why do we want a guru? We say we need a guru because we are confused, and the guru is helpful. He will point out what truth is, he will help us to understand, he knows much more about life than we do, he will act as a father, as a teacher to instruct us in life. He has vast experience and we have little; he will help us through his greater experience, and so on and on. That is, basically, you go to a teacher because you are confused. If you were clear, you would not go near one. Obviously, if you were profoundly happy, if there were no problems, if you understood life completely, you would not go to any guru. I hope you see the significance of this.

Because you are confused, you seek a teacher. You go to him to give you a way of life, to clarify your own confusion, to find truth. You choose your guru because you are confused, and you hope he will give you what you ask. That is, you choose someone who will satisfy your demand; you choose according to the gratification he will give you, and your choice is dependent on your gratification. You do not choose a guru who says to depend on yourself. You choose him according to your prejudices. So since you choose your guru according to the gratification he gives you, you are not seeking truth but a way out of confusion; and the way out of confusion is mistakenly called truth.

Let us examine first this idea that a guru can clear up our confusion. Can anyone else clear up our confusion, which is the product of our responses? We have created it. Do you think someone else has created this misery, this battle at all levels of existence, within and without? It is the result of our own lack of self-knowledge. It is because we do not understand ourselves, our conflicts, our responses, our miseries, that we go to a guru who we think will help us to be free of that confusion. We can understand ourselves only in relationship to the present; and *that relationship itself is the guru*, not someone outside. If I do not understand that relationship, whatever a guru may say is useless, because if I do not understand my relationship to property, to people, to ideas, who can resolve the conflict within me? To resolve that conflict, I must understand it myself, which means I must be aware of myself in relationship. To be aware, no guru is necessary. If I do not know myself, of what use is a guru? Just as a political leader is chosen by those who are in confusion, and whose choice therefore is also confused, so I choose a guru. I can choose him only according to my confusion. Hence, he, like the political leader, is confused.

So what is important is not who is right—whether I am right, or those are who say a guru is necessary—but to find out why you need a guru. Gurus exist for exploitation of various kinds, but that is irrelevant. It gives you satisfaction if someone tells you how you are progressing. But to find out why you need a guru—there lies the key. Another can point out the way; but you have to do all the work, even if you have a guru. Because you do not want to face that, you shift the responsibility to the guru. The guru becomes useless when there is a particle of self-knowledge. No guru, no book or scripture, can give you self-knowledge: it comes when you are aware of yourself in relationship. To be is to be related. Not to understand relationship is misery, strife.

Not to be aware of your relationship to property is one of the causes of confusion. If you do not know your right relationship to property, there is bound to be conflict, which increases the conflict in society. If you do not understand the relationship between you and your wife, between you and your child, how can another resolve the conflict arising out of that relationship? Similarly with ideas, beliefs, and so on. Being confused in your relationship with people, property, and ideas, you seek a guru. If he is a real guru, he will tell you to understand yourself. You are the source of all misunderstanding and confusion; and you can resolve that conflict only when you understand yourself in relationship.

You cannot find truth through anybody else. How can you? Surely, truth is not something static; it has no fixed abode; it is not an end, a goal. On the contrary, it is living, dynamic, alert, alive. How can it be an end? If truth is a fixed point, it is no longer truth; it is then a mere opinion. Truth is the unknown, and a mind that is seeking truth will never find it. For mind is made up of the known, it is the result of the past, the outcome of time—which you can observe for yourself.

Mind is the instrument of the known, hence, it cannot find the unknown; it can only move from the known to the known. When the mind seeks truth, the truth it has read about in books, that 'truth' is self-projected, for then the mind is merely in pursuit of the known, a known more satisfactory than the previous one. When the mind seeks truth, it is seeking its own self-projection, not truth. After all, an ideal is self-projected; it is fictitious, unreal. What is real is what is, not the opposite. But a mind that is seeking reality, seeking God, is seeking the known. When you think of God, your God is the projection of your own thought, the result of social influences. You can think only of the known; you cannot think of the unknown, you cannot concentrate on truth. The moment you think of the unknown, it is merely the self-projected known. So God or truth cannot be thought about. If you think about it, it is not truth. Truth cannot be sought; it comes to you. You can go after only what is known. When the mind is not tortured by the known, by the effects of the known, then only can truth reveal itself. Truth is in every leaf, every tear; it is to be known from moment to moment. No one can lead you to truth; and if anyone leads you, it can only be to the known.

Bombay, 12 March 1950

Questioner: The question of what is truth is an ancient one, and nobody has answered it finally. You speak of truth, but we do not see your experiments or efforts to achieve it, as we saw in the lives of people like Mahatma Gandhi and Dr. Besant. Your pleasant personality is all that we see. Will you explain why there is such a difference between your life and the lives of other seekers of truth. Are there two truths?

Krishnamurti: Do you want proof? And by what standard shall truth be judged? There are those who say that effort and experiment are necessary for truth; but is truth to be gained that way, through trial and error? There are those who struggle and make valiant efforts, who strive spectacularly, either publicly or quietly in caves; and shall they find truth? Is truth a thing to be discovered through effort? Is there a path to truth, your path and my path, the path of the one who makes an effort, and the path of the one who does not? Are there two truths, or has truth many aspects?

Now, this is your problem: You say, 'Certain people—two or several or hundreds—have made efforts, have struggled, have sought truth, whereas you do not make an effort, you lead a pleasant, unassuming life'. So, you want to compare; that is, you have a standard, you have a picture of your leaders who have struggled to achieve truth; and when someone else comes along who does not fit into your frame, you are baffled, and so you ask, 'Which is truth?' You are baffled—that is the important thing, not whether I have truth or someone else has truth. What is important is to find if you can discover reality through effort, will, struggle, striving. Does that bring understanding? Surely, truth is not something distant, but is in the little things of everyday life, in every word, every smile, every relationship, only we do not know how to see it; and the man who tries, struggles valiantly, disciplines, controls himself—will he see truth? The mind that is disciplined, controlled, narrowed down through effort—shall it see truth? Obviously not.

It is only the silent mind that will see the truth, not the mind that makes an effort to see. If you are making an effort to hear what I am saying, will you hear? It is only when you are quiet, when you are really silent, that you understand. If you observe closely, listen quietly, then you will hear; but if you strain, struggle to catch everything that is being said, your energy will be dissipated in that effort. So you will not find truth through effort, it does not matter who says it, whether the ancient books, the ancient saints, or the modern ones. Effort is the very denial of understanding; and it is only the quiet mind, the simple mind, the mind that is still, that is not overtaxed by its own efforts—only such a mind shall understand, shall see truth. Truth is not something in the distance; there is no path to it, there is neither your path nor my path; there is no devotional path, there is no path of knowledge or path of action, because truth has no path to it. The moment you have a path to truth, you divide it, because the path is exclusive; and what is exclusive at the very beginning will end in exclusiveness. The man who is following a path can never know truth because he is living in exclusiveness; his means are exclusive, and the means are the end, are not separate from the end. If the means are exclusive, the end is also exclusive.

So there is no path to truth, and there are not two truths. Truth is not of the past or the present, it is timeless; the man who quotes the truth of the Buddha, of Shankara, of Christ, or who merely repeats what I am saying, will not find truth, because repetition is not truth. Repetition is a lie. Truth is a state of being that arises when the mind that seeks to divide, to be exclusive, that can think only in terms of results, of achievement, has come to an end. Only then will there be truth. The mind that is making effort, disciplining itself in order to achieve an end, cannot know truth, because the end is its own projection, and the pursuit of that projection, however noble, is a form of self-worship. Such a being is worshipping himself, and therefore cannot know truth.

Truth is known only when we understand the whole process of the mind, that is, when there is no strife. Truth is a fact, and the fact can be understood only when the various things that have been placed between the mind and the fact are removed. The fact is your relationship to property, to your wife, to human beings, to nature, to ideas; and as long as you do not understand the fact of relationship, your seeking God merely increases the confusion, because it is a substitution, an escape, and therefore it has no meaning. As long as you dominate your wife or she dominates you, as long as you possess and are possessed, you cannot know love; as long as you are suppressing, substituting, as long as you are ambitious, you cannot know truth. It is not the denial of ambition that makes the mind calm, and virtue is not the denial of evil. Virtue is a state of freedom, of order, which evil cannot give; and the understanding of evil is the establishment of virtue.

The man who builds churches or temples in the name of God with money he has gathered through exploitation, through deceit, through cunning and foul play, will not know truth; he may be mild of tongue, but his tongue is bitter with the taste of exploitation, the taste of sorrow. He alone will know truth who is not seeking, not striving, not trying to achieve a result. The mind itself is a result, and whatever it produces is still a result. But the man who is content with what is shall know truth. Contentment does not mean being satisfied with the status quo, maintaining things as they are—that is not contentment. It is in seeing a fact truly and being free of it, that there is contentment, which is virtue. Truth is not continuous, it has no abiding place, it can be seen only from moment to moment. Truth is always new, and therefore timeless. What was truth yesterday is not truth today, what is truth today is not truth tomorrow. Truth has no continuity. It is the mind that wants to make the experience that it calls truth continuous, and such a mind will not know truth. Truth is always new; it is to see the same smile, and see that smile newly, to see the same person, and see that person anew, to see the waving trees anew, to meet life anew.

Truth is not to be had through books, through devotion, or through self-immolation; it is known when the mind is free, quiet. And that freedom, that quietness of the mind, comes only when the facts of its relationships are understood. Without understanding its relationships, whatever the mind does only creates further problems. But when the mind is free from all its projections, there is a state of quietness in which problems cease, and then only the timeless, the eternal comes into being. Then truth is not a matter of knowledge, it is not a thing to be remembered, it is not something to be repeated, to be printed and spread abroad. Truth is that which is. It is nameless, and so the mind cannot approach it.

London, 23 April 1952

Krishnamurti: For most of us, our whole life is based on effort, some kind of volition. And we cannot conceive of an action that is not based on it. Our social, economic, and so-called spiritual life, is a series of efforts, always culminating in a certain result. We think effort is essential. So we are now going to find out if it is possible to live differently, without this constant battle.

Why do we make effort? Put simply, it is in order to achieve a result, to become something, to reach a goal, isn't it? If we do not make an effort, we think we shall stagnate. We have an idea about the goal towards which we are constantly striving; and this striving has become part of our life. If we want to alter, to bring about a radical change in ourselves, we make a tremendous effort to eliminate old habits, to resist the habitual environmental influences, and so on. So we are used to this series of efforts in order to find or achieve something, in order to live at all.

Now, is not all such effort the activity of the self? Is not effort self-centred activity? And, if we make an effort from the centre of the self, it must inevitably produce more conflict, more confusion, more misery. Yet we keep on making effort after effort; and very few of us realize that the self-centred activity of effort does not clear up any of our problems. On the contrary, it increases our confusion and our misery and our sorrow. Or we know this, and yet continue hoping somehow to break through this self-centred activity of effort, the action of the will.

This is our problem—Is it possible to understand anything without effort? Is it possible to see what is real, what is true, without introducing the action of will, which is essentially based on the self, the 'me?' And if we do not make an effort, is there not a danger of deterioration, of going to sleep, of stagnation? Perhaps, as I am talking, we can experiment with this individually, and see how far we can go through this question. For I feel that what brings happiness, quietness, tranquillity of the mind, does not come through any effort. A truth is not perceived through any volition, through any action of will. And if we can go into it very carefully and diligently, perhaps we shall find the answer.

How do we react when a truth is presented? Take, for example, the problem of fear. We realize that our activity and our being and our whole existence would be fundamentally altered if there were no fear of any kind in us. We may see that, we may see the truth of it; and thereby there is freedom from fear. But for most of us, when a fact, a truth, is put before us, what is our immediate response? Please, experiment with what I am saying; please do not merely listen. Watch your own reactions; and find out what happens when a truth, a fact, is put before you—such as 'any dependency in relationship destroys relationship'. Now, when a statement of that kind is made, what is your response? Do you see, are you aware of, the truth of it, and does dependency thereby cease? Or have you an idea about the fact? Here is a statement of truth. Do we experience the truth of it, or do we create an idea about it?

If we can understand this process of the creation of idea, then we shall perhaps understand the whole process of effort. Because once we have created the idea, then effort comes into being. Then the problem arises, what to do, how to act? That is, we see that psychological dependency on another is a form of self-fulfilment; it is not love; in it there is conflict, fear, the desire to fulfil oneself through another, jealousy, and so on, which corrode. We see that psychological dependency on another embraces all these facts. Then, we proceed to create the idea, do we not? We do not directly experience the fact, the truth of it; but, we look at it, and then create an idea of how to be free from dependency. We see the implications of psychological dependence, and then we create the idea of how to be free from it. We do not directly experience the truth, which is the liberating factor. But out of the experience of looking at that fact we create an idea. We are incapable of looking at it directly, without ideation. Then, having created the idea, we proceed to put that idea into action. Then we try to bridge the gap between idea and action—in which effort is involved.

So can we not look at the truth without creating ideas? It is almost instinctive with most of us: when something true is put before us, we immediately create an idea about it. And I think if we can understand why we do this so instinctively, almost unconsciously, then perhaps we shall understand if it is possible to be free from effort.

Why then do we create ideas about truth? Surely that is important to find out, is it not? Either we see the truth nakedly, as it is, or we do not. But why do we have a picture about it, a symbol, a word, an image, which necessitates a postponement, the hope of an eventual result? So can we hesitantly and guardedly go into this process of why the mind creates the image, the idea—that I must be this or that, that I must be free from dependence, and so on? We know very well that when we see something very clearly, experience it directly, there is a freedom from it. It is that immediacy that is vital, not the picture or the symbol of the truth—on which all systems and philosophies and deteriorating organizations are built. So is it not important to find out why the mind, instead of seeing the thing directly and simply, and experiencing the truth of it immediately, creates an idea about it?

I do not know if you have thought about this. It may perhaps be something new. And to find the truth of it, please do not merely resist. Do not say, 'What would happen if the mind did not create the idea? It is its function to create ideas, to verbalize, to recall memories, to recognize, to calculate'. We know that. But the mind is not free; and it is only when the mind is capable of looking at the truth totally, completely, without any barrier, that there is freedom.

So our problem is—why does the mind, instead of seeing the thing immediately and experiencing it directly, indulge in all these ideas? Is this not one of the habits of the mind? Something is presented to us, and immediately there is the old habit of creating an idea, a theory about it. And the mind likes to live in habit. Because without habit the mind is lost. If there is not a routine, a habitual response to which it has become accustomed, it feels confused, uncertain.

That is one aspect. Also, does not the mind seek a result? Because in the result is permanency. And the mind hates to be uncertain. It is always seeking security in different forms—through beliefs, through knowledge, through experience. And when that is questioned there is a disturbance, anxiety. And so the mind, avoiding uncertainty, seeks security for itself by making efforts to achieve a result.

I hope you are actually observing your own minds in operation. If you are not, then you will not experience, your mind will remain on the verbal level. But—if I may suggest—if you can observe your own mind in operation, and watch how it thinks, how it reacts, when a truth is put before it, then you will experience step-by-step what I am talking about. Then there will be an extraordinary experience. And it is this direct approach, this direct experience of what truth is, that is so essential for bringing about a creative life.

So why does the mind create these ideas, instead of directly experiencing? Why does the mind intervene? As we have said, it is habit. Also, the mind wants to achieve a result. We all want to achieve a result. In listening to me, are you looking for a result? You are, aren't you? The mind is seeking a result; it sees that dependency is destructive, and therefore it wants to be free of it. But the very desire to be free creates the idea. The mind is not free; but the desire to be free creates the idea of freedom as the goal towards which it must work. And thereby effort comes into being. And that effort is self-centred; it does not bring freedom. Instead of depending on a person, you depend on an idea or on an image. So your effort is only self-enclosing; it is not liberating.

Now, can the mind, realizing that it is caught in habit, be free from habit—not have an idea that it should achieve freedom as an eventual goal, but see the truth that the mind is caught in habit, directly experience it? And similarly, can the mind see that it is pursuing incessantly a permanency for itself, a goal that it must achieve, a God, a truth, a virtue, a state of being, or whatever, and is thereby bringing about this action of will, with all its complications? And when we see that, is it not possible to experience the truth of something *directly* without all the paraphernalia of verbalization? You may objectively see a fact, in that there is no ideation, no creation of idea, symbol, desire. But subjectively, inwardly, it is entirely different. Because there we want a result; there is the craving to be something, to achieve, to become—in which all effort is born.

I feel that to see what is true from moment to moment, without any effort, but directly to experience it, is the only creative existence. Because it is only in moments of complete tranquillity that you discover something—not when you are making an effort, whether it is under the microscope or inwardly. It is only when the mind is not agitated, not caught in habit, not trying to achieve a result, not trying to become something—it is only when it is not doing these things, when it is really tranquil, when there is no effort, no movement—that there is a possibility of discovering something new.

Surely, that is freedom from the self, that is the abnegation of the 'me'—and not the outward symbols, whether you possess this or that virtue or not. But freedom comes into being only when you understand your own processes, conscious as well as unconscious. It is possible only when we go fully into the different processes of the mind. And as most of us live in a state of tension, in constant effort, it is essential to understand the complexity of effort, to see the truth that effort does not bring virtue, that effort is not love, that effort does not bring about the freedom that truth alone can give—which is a direct experiencing. For that, one has to understand the mind, one's own mind—not somebody else's mind, not what somebody else says about it. You may read all the volumes ever written but they will be utterly useless. For you must observe your own mind, and penetrate it more and more deeply, and experience the thing directly as you go along. Because *there* is the living quality, not in the things of the mind. And the mind, to find its own processes, must not be enclosed by its own habits, but must be free occasionally to look. Therefore, it is important to understand this whole process of effort. For effort does not bring about freedom. Effort is only more and more self-enclosing, more and more destructive, outwardly as well as inwardly, in relationship with one or with many.

Questioner: I find that a group that meets regularly to discuss your teachings tends to become confusing and boring. Is it better to think over these things alone, or with others?

K: What is important? Isn't it to find out, to discover for yourself the things about yourself? If that is your urgent, immediate, instinctive necessity, then you can do it with one or with many, by yourself or with two or three. But when that is lacking, groups become boring. Then people who come to the group are dominated by one or two of its members, who know everything, who are in immediate contact with the person who has already said these things. So the one becomes the authority, and gradually exploits the many. We know this all too familiar game. But people submit to it because they like being together. They like to talk, to have the latest gossip or the latest news. And so the thing soon deteriorates. You start with a serious intention, and it becomes something ugly.

But if we really, insistently, feel the need to discover for ourselves what is true, then all relationship becomes important. But such people are rare. Because we are not really serious; and so we eventually make of groups and organizations something to be avoided. Surely it depends on whether you are really earnest to discover these things for yourself. And this discovery can come at any moment—not only in a group, or only when you are by yourself, but whenever you are aware of and sensitive to the intimations of your own being. To watch yourself—the way you talk at table, the way you talk to your neighbour, your subordinate, your boss—surely all these, if one is aware, indicate the state of your own being. And it is that discovery which is important. Because it is that discovery which liberates.

Q: What is the most creative way of meeting great grief and loss?

K: What do we mean by *meeting?* We mean, how to approach it, what we should do about it, how to conquer it, how to be free of it, how to derive benefit from it, how to learn from it so as to avoid more suffering? Surely that is what we mean by how to *meet* grief.

Now, what do we mean by *grief?* Is it something apart from us? Is it something outside of us, inwardly or outwardly, which we are observing, which we are experiencing? Are we merely the observers experiencing? Or is grief something different? Surely that is an important point. When I say, 'I suffer', what do I mean by it? Am I different from the suffering? Surely that is the question. Let us find out.

There is sorrow—I am not loved or my son dies. There is one part of me that is demanding the explanation, the reasons, the causes. The other part of me is in agony for various reasons. And there is also another part of me that wants to be free from the sorrow, that wants to go beyond it. We are all these things, are we not? So, if one part of me is rejecting and resisting sorrow, another part of me is seeking an explanation, is caught up in theories, and another part of me is escaping from the fact, how then can I understand it totally? It is only when I am capable of integrated understanding that there is a possibility of freedom from sorrow. But if I am torn in different directions, then I do not see the truth of it.

So it is very important to find out whether I am merely the observer experiencing sorrow. If I am merely the observer experiencing sorrow, then there are two states in my being—the one who observes, who thinks, who experiences, and the other who is observed, which is the experience, the thought. So as long as there is a division there is no immediate freedom from sorrow.

Now, please listen carefully and you will see that when there is a fact, a truth, there is understanding of it only when I can experience the whole thing without division—and not when there is a separation of the 'me' observing suffering. That is the truth. Now, what is your immediate reaction to that? Is not your immediate reaction, response, 'How am I to bridge the gap between the two?' I recognize that there are different entities in me—the thinker and the thought, the experiencer and the experience, the one who suffers and the one who observes the suffering. As long as there is a division, a separation, there is conflict. And it is only when there is integration that there is freedom from sorrow. That is the truth, that is the fact. Now, how do you respond to it? Do you see the thing immediately, and experience it directly, or do you ask the question, 'How am I to bridge the division between the two entities? How am I to bring about integration?' Is that not your instinctive response? If that is so, then you are not seeing the truth. Your question of how to bring about integration has no value. For it is only when I can see the thing completely, wholly, without this division in myself, that there is a possibility of freedom from the thing that I call sorrow.

So one has to find out how one looks at sorrow. Not what the books or what anybody else says, not according to any teacher or authority, but how you regard it, how you instinctively approach it. Then you will surely find out if there really is this division in your mind. So long as there is that division, there must be sorrow. So long as there is the desire to be free from sorrow, to resist sorrow, to seek explanations, to avoid, then sorrow becomes the shadow, everlastingly pursuing.

So what is very important in this question is how each one of us responds to psychological pain—when we are bereaved, when we are hurt, and so on. We need not go here into the causes of sorrow. But we know them very well—the ache of loneliness; the fear of losing, of not being loved; being frustrated; the loss of someone. We are only too familiar with this thing called sorrow. And we have many very convenient and satisfying explanations. But explanations do not bring freedom from sorrow. They may cover up, but the thing continues. And we are trying to find out how to be free from sorrow, not which explanations are more satisfactory. There can be such freedom only if there is an integration. And we cannot understand what integration is unless we are first aware of how we look at sorrow.

Q: For one who is caught in habit it seems impossible to see the truth of a thing instantaneously. Surely time is needed—time to break away from one's immediate activity and really seek to go into what has been happening?

K: Now what do we mean by *time?* Please—again let us experiment. Obviously not time by the clock. When you say, 'I need time', what does it mean? That you need leisure—an hour to yourself, or a few minutes to yourself? Surely you do not mean that? You mean, 'I need time to achieve a result'. That is, 'I need time to break away from the habits that I have created'.

Now, time is obviously the product of the mind; mind is the result of time. What we think, feel, our memories, are basically the result of time. And you say that time is necessary to break away from certain habits. That is, this inward psychological habit is the outcome of desire and fear, is it not? I see the mind is caught in it, and I say, 'I need time to break it down. I realize it is this habit that is preventing me from seeing things immediately, experiencing them directly, and so I must have time to break down this habit'.

First, how does habit come into being? Through education, through environmental influences, through our own memories. Also, it is comfortable to have a mechanism that functions habitually, so that it is never uncertain, quivering, inquiring, doubtful, anxious. So, the mind creates the pattern that we call habit, routine. And in that it functions. And the questioner wants to know how to break down that habit, so that experience can be direct. You see what has happened?

The moment we say How? we have already introduced the idea of time. But if we can see that the mind creates habits, and functions in habit, and that a mind enclosed by its own self-created memories, desires, and fears cannot see or experience anything directly—when we can see the truth of that, then there is a possibility of experiencing directly. The perception of truth is obviously not a matter of time. That is one of the conveniences of the mind—that eventually, next life, I shall reach perfection, whatever I want. So being caught, the mind then proceeds to say How am I to be free? It can never *get* free. It can *be* free only when it sees the truth of how it creates habit by tradition, by cultivating virtues in order to be something, by seeking to have permanency, to have security. All these things are barriers. In that state, how can the mind see or experience anything directly? If we see that it cannot, then there is *immediate* freedom. But the difficulty is, of course, that most of us like to continue in our habits of thought and feeling, our traditions, beliefs, hopes. Surely, the mind is made up of all those things. How can such a mind experience anything that is not its own projection? Obviously it cannot. So it can only understand its own mechanism and see the truth of its own activities. And then there is freedom from that, then there is direct experience.

Talk to Students at Rajghat, 31 December 1952

MOST OF US are concerned with doing a little bit of change here and there, and we are satisfied with that. As we grow older, we do not want any deep, fundamental change, because we are afraid. We do not think in terms of transformation, we think only in terms of change; and you will find, when you look into it, that it is only a modified change, which is not a radical revolution, not a transformation. You have to face all these things, from your own happiness to the happiness of the many, from your own self-seeking pursuits and ambitions to the ambitions and the motives and the pursuits of others; you have to face competition, the corruption in oneself and in others, the deterioration of the mind, the emptiness of the heart. You have to know all this, you have to face all this, but you are not prepared for it.

What do we know when we leave here? We are as dull, empty, and shallow as when we came in; and our studies, our living in school, our contacts with our teachers and their contact with us have not helped us to understand this very complex problem of life. The teachers are dull, and we become dull like them. They are afraid and we are afraid. So it is our problem, it is your problem as well as the teachers' problem, to see that you go out with maturity, with thought, without fear, so that you will be able to face life intelligently. It appears very important to find an answer to all these problems, *but there is no answer.* All you can do is meet these very complex problems intelligently as they arise. Please understand this. You want an answer. You think that by reading, by following somebody, by studying some book, you will find an answer to all these very complex and subtle problems. But you will not find answers, because these problems have been created by human beings who may have been like you. The starvation, the cruelty, the hideousness, the squalor, the appalling callousness, the cruelty—all this has been created by human beings.

So you have to understand the human heart, the human mind, which is yourself. Merely looking for an answer in a book, or going to a school to find out, or following an economic system, however much it may promise, or following some religious absurdity and superstition, following a guru, or rituals, will in no way help you to understand these problems, because they are created by you and others like you. As they are created by you, you cannot understand them without understanding yourself; and to understand yourself, as you live, from moment to moment, from day to day, year in and year out, you need intelligence, a great deal of insight, love, and patience.

Bombay, 8 February 1953

Questioner: Often we feel abandoned by you. We know you have not accepted us as disciples, but need you shirk your responsibility towards us completely? Should you not see us through?

Krishnamurti: This is a roundabout way of asking, 'Why don't you become our guru?' (laughter). Now, the problem is not abandoning or seeing you through, because we are supposed to be grown-up people. Physically we are grown-up; mentally we are the age of fourteen and fifteen; and we want a glorified somebody, a saviour, a guru, a master, to lead us out of our misery and confusion; to explain our chaotic state to us; to explain it, not to bring about a revolution in our thinking, but to explain it away. That is what we are concerned with.

When you put this question, you want to find a way out of confusion, to be free from fear, from hatred, from all the pettiness of life; and you look to somebody to help you. Other gurus have perhaps not succeeded in putting you to sleep with a dose of opium, an explanation, so you turn to this person and say, 'Please help us through'. Is that our problem—the substitution of a new guru for an old one, of a new master for an old one, of a new leader for the old? Please listen to this carefully. Can anybody lead you to truth, to the discovery of truth? Is discovery possible when you are led to it, have you experienced it? Can anybody—it does not matter who—lead you to truth? When you say you must follow somebody, does it not imply that truth is stationary, that truth is there for you to be led to, for you to look at and take?

Is truth something that you are led to? If it is, then the problem is very simple; you will find the most satisfying guru or leader and he will lead you to it. But surely the truth of that something you are seeking is beyond the state of explanation. It is not static, it must be experienced, be discovered, and you cannot experience it through guidance. How can I experience spontaneously something original if I am told, 'This is original, experience it'? Hatred, meanness, ambition, and pettiness are the problems, and not the discovery of what truth is. You cannot find what truth is with a petty mind. A mind that is shallow, gossiping, stupid, ambitious—such a mind can never find what truth is. A petty mind will create only a petty thing, it will be empty, it will create a shallow God. So our problem now is not to find, to discover what God is, but first to see how petty we are.

Look, if I know that I am petty, miserable, unhappy, then I can deal with it. But if I say, 'I must not be petty, I must be great', then I am running away—which is pettiness.

What is important is to understand and discover what is, not to transform what is into something else. After all, a stupid mind, even if it is trying to become very cunning, clever, intelligent, is still stupid because its very essence is stupidity. We do not listen. We want somebody to lead our pettiness to something bigger and we never accept, never see, what is, what actually is. The discovery of what is, the actuality, is important; it is the only thing that matters. At any level—economic, social, religious, political, psychological—what is important is to discover exactly what is, not what should be.

Poona, 10 September 1958

You have to find out what the speaker has to say before you accept, reject, or criticize. First you have to find out what he means, what he intends. He may exaggerate, he may not give the right emphasis, but you have to take all that in by listening. Then you and I can establish a right relationship. I have something to say that I think will upset the applecart, the tradition, all those things. But before you have found out what is actually being said, please do not begin to build a defensive barrier. Keep your reactions to what I have to say until later, when you will have the right to criticize, to discard, to accept or to go into it, as you will. But until then I suggest to you that you do not quickly react. Listen in a friendly manner, but with a clear mind, not accepting or rejecting or taking what I say and opposing it by quoting some authority, because I do not believe in authorities.

Truth is not come to by authority. It must be discovered from moment to moment. It is not a permanent thing, enduring, continuous. It must be found each minute, each second. That requires a great deal of attention, a great alertness of mind, and you cannot understand it or allow it to come to you if you merely quote authorities, merely speculate as to whether there is or is not God. You must experience it as an individual, or rather, allow that thing to come to you. You cannot possibly go to it.

Please let us be clear on this point, that you cannot by any process, through any discipline, through any form of meditation, go to truth, God, or whatever name you like to give it. It is much too vast, it cannot possibly be conceived of; no description will cover it, no book can hold it, nor any word contain it. So you cannot by any devious method, by any sacrifice, by any discipline or through any guru, go to it. You must await it, it will come to you, you cannot go to it. That is the fundamental thing one has to understand, that not through any trick of the mind, not through any control, through any virtue, any compulsion, any form of suppression, can the mind possibly go to truth.

All that the mind can do is be quiet—but not with the intention of receiving it. And that is one of the most difficult things of all because we think truth can be experienced right away through doing certain things. Truth is not to be bought any more than love can be bought. And if you and I understand that very clearly from the very beginning, then what I have to say will have a very different, a very definite, meaning. Otherwise you will be in a state of self-contradiction. You think there is truth, God, a state that is permanent, and you want it, so you practise discipline, do various forms of exercise, but it cannot be bought. Any amount of devotion, sacrifice, knowledge, or virtue cannot call it into being. The mind must be free, it must have no borders, no frontier, no limitation, no conditioning. The whole sense of acquisitiveness must come to an end, but not in order to receive.

If one really understood that, one would see what an extraordinary thing this creativity of the mind is. Then you would really understand how to free the mind so that it is in a state of alert watchfulness, never asking, never seeking, never demanding.

As I have said, I am talking to the individual because only the individual can change, not the mass; only you can transform yourself, and so the individual matters infinitely. I know it is the fashion to talk about groups, the mass, the race, as though the individual has no importance at all, but in any creative action it is the individual who matters. Any true action, any important decision, the search for freedom, the inquiry after truth, can only come from the individual who understands. That is why I am talking only to the individual. You will probably say, 'What can I, the individual do?' Confronted with this enormous complication, the national and religious divisions, the problems of misery, starvation, war, unemployment, the rapid degradation and disintegration, what can one individual do about it all? Nothing.

The individual cannot tackle the mountain outside, but the individual can set a new current of thought going that will create a different series of actions. He cannot do anything about worldwide conditions because historical events must take their own brutal, cruel, indifferent course. But if there were half a dozen people who could think completely about the whole problem, they would set going a different attitude and action altogether, and that is why the individual is so important. But if he wants to reform this enormous confusion, this mountain of disintegration, he can do very little; indeed, as is being shown, he can have no effect on it at all, but if any one of us is truly individual in the sense that he is trying to understand the whole process of his mind, then he will be a creative entity, a free person, unconditioned, capable of pursuing truth for itself and not for a result.

So, as I have said, that reality of which the mind cannot possibly conceive, which it cannot possibly speculate upon or reduce to words, that truth must come to you, the individual. You cannot go to it. After all, it is fairly obvious that the individual mind, which is also the collective mind, is narrow, petty, brutal, ugly, selfish, arrogant. How can such a mind invite the unknown? For whatever it thinks must be petty, small—even as its Gods are. Your God is the invention of the mind. You may put a garment round it but its garments are yours; it is your God, but it is not truth, it is not reality. Do what you will, reality cannot be invited; it must come to you. So what is one to do?

How is one to experience that something that is not merely created by the mind? That is possible only when the mind begins to understand its own process, its own ways. I am using the word *process* not in the sense of a means to an end. Generally we mean by the word *process* that if you do certain things there will be a result—if you put oil in the machine it will run properly, if you follow certain disciplines, make sacrifices, you will get something in return. I am not using the word in that sense at all. I am using the word *process* to mean the operation of the mind as it works, not as it searches for a result.

So the mind must come to the state when it is free from all effort, and I want to discuss the whole problem of effort and conflict and whether there is a state that the mind can reach without conflict in order to arrive at the truth. For it is only when the mind ceases to be in self-contradiction, and therefore ceases to be in conflict, that it is capable of looking and of understanding. It is fairly clear that a mind in conflict can never understand anything, and so we want to find out why the mind is in a state of self-contradiction. Surely, if we can understand the conflict within the mind itself we shall go very far, because it will reveal why there is this contradiction within oneself. If we can go slowly, step-by-step, into that question and if you really follow it, not oppose it, then perhaps you will come to a state of mind in which there is no conflict at all. But you cannot just accept my words, for it means that you also must work, not merely listen, that you must become aware of the operation of your own mind. I am only explaining, but it is for you to watch your own mind in operation.

So first of all, why is there conflict in our lives? We generally take it for granted that it must be so, that it is inevitable, that man is born in conflict; and we try to find ways and means to overcome it. In relationships, in the political or any other sphere, there is a conflict within, which brings about self-contradiction; there is also the outward contradiction between what we feel we should be and what we are. I want to find out why this contradiction exists. I do not accept that it is natural, inevitable, that there is no solution for it and so we must escape from it. That is immature thinking. I want to understand it, and so I will not escape from it, dodge it, or go to a guru or a cinema. To me, turning to a book, going to a guru, or going into deep meditation when you are in conflict are just the same as taking to drink. But I want to understand if one can remove this inward contradiction. If that is clear we can proceed from there, and please do not say at the end, 'Why did you not talk about birth control' or, 'I came here to find out what religion is, if there is a God'.

A contradictory mind cannot find anything whatsoever of the truth. Just think of it—how can you, being in contradiction, know anything that is not contradictory? How can you possibly know that state which has no opposites, no divisions, which is the immeasurable? This question you will answer for yourself, and find the truth of, only when you find out if you can eliminate contradiction within yourself. And that is essential. What you are seeking at present is not the elimination of contradiction, but peace for yourself, some state in which the mind will not be disturbed at all. It is like sitting on a volcano and saying, 'Let me have peace'. There is no meaning to it. So I say: let us examine what is in the volcano, let it come out, the ugly, the bestial, the loveliness, everything—let it come up and let me look at it, which means that the mind must have no fear. So let us go into it.

Now why is there this state of contradiction in us? Let us begin at the lowest level. I want money, and also I do not want money because I think that it is good to be poor. I am not talking of the man who wholeheartedly says, 'I want to be rich'—and goes after it; to him there is no contradiction. He is full of energy because he is aggressive, brutal, ruthless, corrupt, violent; he wants money, he wants position; so there is no conflict within. In Hitler, Khrushchev, and all the leaders of the world, there is no consciousness of contradiction because they want this thing and go after it, by right means or crooked. We would like to be in that position also but unfortunately we are not. We are in contradiction and want a state of mind that will be permanently peaceful and have no contradiction. Or take the man who is somewhat insane. To him there is no conflict because he simply says, 'I am God' or

'I am Napoleon', or he identifies himself with some other belief and so there is no sense of contradiction. He is what he imagines, and being that, he is full of energy.

Have you not noticed such people? They will travel up and down the land, doing this and doing that, because they are completely taken up with an idea, completely absorbed. And we would also like to be in that state. So we pursue various ideas until we find something that will suit us, and there we stop. So we must ask again: why is there in us this contradiction? Contradiction is conflict, is it not? If I am greedy and I do not want to be greedy, there is immediately a state of contradiction in me that brings conflict. But if I am completely greedy there is no conflict. Or if I am completely non-greedy, there is no conflict. But why is there this contradiction that, if we are intelligent, if our mind is alert, becomes ever stronger and stronger and is not easily gotten rid of? The stronger, the more active, the more passionate one is, the more energetic one becomes, and the contradiction becomes ever greater until, having established a deep, lasting contradiction, we try to escape from it by saying that life is a process of disintegration and disillusionment, and we philosophize indefinitely. Whereas I think this contradiction can be totally removed, not partly but totally. When you love something, when you are interested in something, there is no effort in the sense of working at it.

For most of us work is effort; going to the office, doing various things you do not want to do, disciplining yourself, which means work, which means effort. But if you can go beyond the words we are using to understand this contradiction, you will find a state of being without effort. Let us look at violence and non-violence. We are violent and we say we must not be violent. Non-violence is the ideal; it is the projection of the mind that feels itself to be violent. So you make non-violence into an ideal and then proceed to try to transform violence into that ideal. But the non-violence has no reality! No ideal has any reality, obviously. You do not easily agree with me at first because it is very difficult to eject ideas and ideals from the mind, which means that your mind is so conditioned by ideals that a new idea cannot be received by it. You are as mesmerized by the ideal as the lunatic by his idea. I am not insulting you; I am just saying how difficult it is for a mind that thinks in habits to consider a new idea. We can see very clearly how ideals are created. I am something—violent, greedy, or what you will—and I want to transform that into the so-called ideal, the opposite. So I create the opposite ideal to what I actually am and begin to have an infinite variety of conflicts. I am this and I must be that; this is the source of conflict. The moment the mind says: I am not but I must be, you have begun the whole process of conflict.

Most of you will think that if you do not make an effort you will go to seed, vegetate, and that if there were no pressure, conflict, compulsion, you would become like a cow. Therefore, you bring up your children—as does society, the whole world—geared to the effort to become something, which involves this perpetual movement of conflict. So I can see that there must be conflict so long as there is an ideal, and that so long as the mind is concerned with the future, with what should be, it is not concerned with what is. It is fairly obvious that one cannot have a divided mind, part of the mind occupied with non-violence and the other part occupied with violence. Therefore, you see that so long as there is any kind of ideal in the mind there must be a state of contradiction. This does not mean that you can merely accept what is, and just stagnate.

The real revolution begins when you can put away all your ideals—and how difficult that is! You have been brought up with ideals. All the books, the saints, the professors, the erudite people, everyone has said that you must have ideals, and that thought has become a habit. It is purely a habit. You are holding on to so many lovely ideals, and when someone comes along and tells you how absurd these ideals are, how they have no reality at all, then for the mind to really see that that is so is to know the truth. Truth is not something away over the hills and mountains. It is the perception of the true in simple things, and if you see the truth of what we have been saying now, you will break the habit of ideals.

But for centuries we have been brought up on ideals—the ideal that you must become something, either an executive or the prime minister; and if you cannot be one of these you turn towards becoming a saint. You are always wanting to become something, either in this world or in the so-called spiritual world. So you have ideals for here and ideals for there. And therefore you have set up a vast field of conflict, which is habit. It has become such a strong, impregnable habit, and you have not thought it out.

It is a very difficult habit to break because you are fearful of what is going to happen. Your relationship with people will change; you will no longer easily accept everything that everybody has said. You will begin to question. You might lose your job. So fear steps in and dictates. Fear says: Do not give up these things because what is going to happen then? Your wife believes in ideals and if you give them up there are going to be perpetual quarrels in the house. Who are you to go against the whole authority that has been set up? What right have you to do so? So society smothers you. And unconsciously you are frightened, and you say, 'Please, I will only accept these ideals verbally, as I know they have no meaning'. But you have not solved the problem of conflict.

Conflict arises, does it not, because man has never tackled the problem of what is, irrespective of what should be. To understand what is requires a great deal of attention, intense search, intense inquiry; but to follow an ideal is very easy—and it does not mean a thing. But if you say, 'I am violent and I am going to disregard all the idealistic nonsense about non-violence and understand the violence', your position is clear. Then the question arises, since you are free of the ideal, will you no longer seek to change what is? Previously the ideal acted as a lever with which you sought to change what is. You thought the idea of non-violence acted as an influence by which you could get rid of violence. That is, having created contradiction through the ideal, we hope, through conflict, to get rid of violence. But we have never succeeded in doing that. It goes with brutality, outwardly or suppressed, and produces its own results. So can I be left only with violence, not holding on also to its opposite? If so, I have removed one of the causes of conflict, perhaps the major cause.

To be free of ideals is most difficult, for you may remove them outwardly, but still have inward ideals—the so-called inward experience, which tells you what to do. You may reject outward authority, and fairly intelligent people have done that, but inwardly they still want to be something, not only the boss of the town or the school, they also want to be spiritual, to achieve a state of mind that is at perfect peace. But the desire to be at peace indicates that you are not at peace, so you have to tackle what is actual. So you see the complex nature of contradiction! Though you may consciously say how absurd these ideals are, they are embedded in the unconscious. Our whole race is steeped in ideals. It is not a matter of just removing a few silly ones, you have to understand the whole process of the mind.

One of the difficulties for most of us is that we do not seem to be able to see the whole. We only see the part. Do not at once say, 'How am I to see the whole?' That is not the problem. The problem is that our minds are so small that we do not seem able to take in the whole at one glance. We cannot see the whole mountain, because our minds, being small, being petty, are occupied with details, and a collection of details does not make the whole. Please ask yourself why your mind does not receive the truth totally free of the falseness of the whole process of idealization. Must we go through the removal of each ideal, one by one? This would be an enormous task, wouldn't it? Day after day, struggling, tearing them out; it would take years, surely, to go step by step taking one ideal after another and discarding it. So can I not see the whole simple truth that ideals are totally unnecessary? Can I not see the immense significance of it in a flash, and let that truth that I have seen operate?

You all know the truth that a cobra bites and you might die from it. That is a fact. So what do you do? When you go into the woods and walk at night you are naturally very careful. You do not have to say, 'I must think about cobras'. The fear of being bitten is operating in you. Or in your bathroom you may have a bottle marked poison. The liquid is poisonous and that is a fact. And so, without thinking, your mind is always alert, even in the dark, and you do not take the bottle and drink. You know the truth that the poison in the cobra and the bottle are dangerous and your mind is alert to it, not just for one moment but all the time. Similarly, if you can see the truth that ideals have no reality, see it right through, completely, then the perception of the total truth that ideals have no value will begin to operate of itself. *You* do not have to operate. *It* will operate.

If you see the truth of that, then you do not have to make an effort to break the ideals one by one. The truth will do it. So the point I want to make is: Can you not see the totality of the truth of something immediately, as you see the truth that a cobra is poisonous? If you see the truth that conflict must cease, and that conflict is brought about through this division between what I think I should be and what I am, then you do not have to do a thing. Your conscious mind cannot deal with the imponderable unconscious, but the truth that you have seen will do so. Has this happened to you? That is, do you see the truth of all this; not all the implications of it, because that is merely a matter of exploration and time. If you feel the truth of it then for the moment let us leave it aside and tackle the problem of 'what is', because our whole endeavour is to eliminate self-contradiction.

With most people, the more tension there is in contradiction the more active they are. There is tension in contradiction. I am violent and I must not be violent; that opposition creates a tension, and from that tension you act, write a book, or try to do something about it. That is our entire activity at present. You say in India that you are a non-violent race. God knows what it means! For you are preparing an army and spending 37 percent of your money on it, I was told. And look what it is doing to you, not only to the poor people but to the race. You say one thing and do quite the opposite. Why? Because, you say, 'If we had no army, Pakistan would attack', and Pakistan says the same nonsense, and so you keep up this game. Not only in India but throughout the world it is the same contradiction—we are all kind, loving people and preparing for war! So this nation, this race, the group, the family, the individual, is in a state of contradiction, and the more intense the contradiction the greater the tension, and the greater the tension the greater the activity. The activity takes different forms, from writing a book to becoming a hermit. So each one of us is somewhat schizophrenic, in a state of contradiction. And not knowing how to get away from it we turn to religion, or take drugs, or chase women, or go to the temple—any form of activity that takes us away from what is. We reform the village but we never tackle this fundamental thing.

So I want to tackle 'what is', because otherwise I see that I will always be in contradiction. A man at peace within himself needs no gods because then he can go very deeply into himself, and very far, where frontiers of recognition have completely stopped. And those frontiers must end before the mind can receive that which is eternal. Do not just agree, because this is one of the most difficult things to do and requires tremendous work on yourself. That work is not effort. It becomes an effort, a conflict, a contradiction only when you still want to become something.

So I want to examine 'what is', which is that I am greedy, I am violent. I am examining that and I see that there must be no contradictory approach to it. I must look at what I am and understand it, but not in relation to what should be. Can I do that? Again you will find that it is one of the most difficult things to do—to examine what is without judgement, without comparison, without acceptance, without condemnation, because the moment you condemn you enter the field of contradiction. So can you and I look at violence without introducing the element that creates contradiction, the element of either acceptance or denial. So can I look at my violence? What is the state of the mind that, having eliminated contradiction, looks at that violence? I am left only with that which is actual, am I not—with the simple fact that I am violent, greedy, or sexual? Can I look at it?

What is the state of the mind that looks at a fact? Have you ever really looked at any fact—a woman, a man, a child, a flower, a sunset? What do you do when you look? You are thinking of something else, are you not? You say, that is a handsome man and I must not look at him, or that is a beautiful woman and I wish she were my wife. You never look without a reaction. You look at a sunset and merely say how lovely it is or that it is not as beautiful as it was yesterday. So you have never looked at it. Your memory of yesterday destroys the perception of what is today. How extraordinarily difficult it is for us to look at something clearly, openly, simply! Now let us look at another fact. Why are you listening to me? You are listening to me, obviously, because I have a reputation. You think I can do something for you. You think you must listen to me either because intellectually it amuses you or for some other reason, and so you are not actually listening. What is actually happening is, that since what I say contradicts what you think, you do not listen. All you are listening to is what you think you know about me—and you do not really know a thing! What is important is not to know about me, but to really follow what is being said, to find out if it has any basis, any reality, any sense, or whether it is nonsense, false. That is the only important thing, and what you think about me personally is totally irrelevant.

So I ask, have you ever looked at a fact? Please, when you go home really try it, just for fun. If you have a flower in your room look at it, and see what the mind does. See whether the mind can took at it, or whether it immediately says: it is a rose, or it has faded, and so on. You can, perhaps, look at a flower, at your wife or child, but it is much more difficult to look at yourself, totally, to watch yourself without introducing the factor of contradiction or acceptance. Can I just look at my violence without any form of acceptance or denial? You will see, if you try, how extraordinarily difficult it is, because the habit comes in and says all kinds of things. Looking at a fact, whether a political fact, a religious fact, or the fact of starvation, requires attention, not a state of contradiction. There can be no attention if there is contradiction.

There is starvation in many parts of the world, perhaps not in America, Europe, or Russia, but all over Asia. Everybody talks about it and nothing happens. Why? The Communists, the Socialists, the reformers, and the big politicians all talk about it, all the world talks and yet nothing happens. The fact is that there is starvation, and another fact is that each group wants the solution of starvation to be according to its own system and says, 'My system is better than yours'. Because there are national divisions, the manipulation of power politics, this goes on and on. So the fact is that nobody wants to tackle the problem of starvation. They merely want to act in their own way. These are all facts. So can you find out how the mind looks at a fact? Your approach to the fact is far more important than the fact itself because if you approach it rightly the fact undergoes a tremendous change.

From Truth and Actuality, *Brockwood Park, 18 May 1975*

Krishnamurti: I was thinking about the question of what truth is and what reality is and whether there is any relationship between the two, or whether they are separate. Are they eternally divorced, or are they just projections of thought? And if thought didn't operate, would there be reality? I thought that reality comes from *res*, thing, and that anything that thought operates on, or fabricates, or reflects on, is reality. And thought, thinking in a distorted, conditioned manner, is illusion, is self-deception, is distortion. I left it there, because I wanted to let it come rather than my pursuing it.

David Bohm: The question of thought and reality and truth has occupied philosophers over the ages. It's a very difficult one. It seems to me that what you say is basically true, but there are a lot of points that need to be ironed out. One of the questions that arises **is** this: If reality is thought, does what thought thinks about, what appears in consciousness, go beyond consciousness?

K: Are the contents of consciousness reality?

DB: That's the question; and can we use thought as equivalent to consciousness in its basic form?

K: Yes.

DB: I wonder whether, just for the sake of completeness, we should also include in thought feeling, desire, will, and reaction. I feel we should, if we are exploring the connection between consciousness, reality, and truth.

K: Yes.

DB: One of the points I'd like to bring up is: There is thought, there is our consciousness, and there is the thing of which we are conscious. And as you have often said, the thought is not the thing.

K: Yes.

DB: We have to get it clear, because in some sense the thing may have some kind of reality independent of thought; we can't go so far as to deny all that. Or do we go as far as some philosophers, like Bishop Berkeley, who has said that all is thought? Now I would like to suggest a possibly useful distinction between that reality which is largely created by our own thought, or by the thought of mankind, and that reality which one can regard as existing independently of this thought. For example, would you say nature is real?

K: It is, yes.

DB: And it is not just our own thoughts.

K: No, obviously not.

DB: The tree, the whole earth, the stars.

K: Of course, the cosmos.

DB: Yes. I was thinking the other day, illusion is real, in the sense that it is really something going on, to a person who is in a state of illusion.

K: To him it is real.

DB: But to us it is also real because his brain is in a certain state of electrical and chemical movement, and he acts from his illusion in a real way.

K: In a real way, in a distorted way.

DB: Distorted but real. Now it occurred to me that one could say that even the false is real but not true. This might be important.

K: I understand. For instance: Is Christ real?

DB: He is certainly real in the minds of people who believe in him, in the sense we have been discussing.

K: We want to find out the distinction between truth and reality. We said anything that thought thinks about, whether unreasonably or reasonably, is a reality. It may be distorted or reasoned clearly, it is still a reality. That reality, I say, has nothing to do with truth.

DB: Yes, but we have to say besides, that in some way reality involves more than mere thought. There is also the question of actuality. Is the thing actual? Is its existence an actual fact? According to the dictionary, the fact means what is actually done, what actually happens, what is actually perceived.

K: Yes, we must understand what we mean by the fact.

DB: The fact is the action that is actually taking place. Suppose, for example, that you are walking on a dark road and that you think you see something. It may be real, it may not be real. One moment you feel that it's real and the next moment that it's not real. But then you suddenly touch it and it resists your movement. From this action it's immediately clear that there is a real thing that you have contacted. But if there is no such contact you say that it's not real, that it was perhaps an illusion, or at least something mistakenly taken as real.

K: But, of course, that thing is still a reality that thought thinks about. And reality has nothing to do with truth.

DB: But now, let us go further with the discussion of 'the thing'. You see, the root of the English word *thing* is fundamentally the same as the German *bedingen*, to condition, to set the conditions or determine. And indeed we must agree that a thing is necessarily conditioned.

K: It is conditioned. Let's accept that.

DB: This is a key point. Any form of reality is conditioned. Thus, illusion is still a form of reality that is conditioned. For example, the man's blood may have a different constitution because he's not in a balanced state. He is distorting, he may be too excited, and that could be why he is caught in illusion. So every thing is determined by conditions and it also conditions every other thing.

K: Yes, quite.

DB: All things are interrelated in the way of mutual conditioning, which we call influence. In physics that's very clear—the planets all influence one another, the atoms influence one another, and I wanted to suggest that maybe we could regard thought and consciousness as part of this whole chain of influence.

K: Quite right.

DB: So that every thing can influence consciousness, and it in turn can work back and influence the shapes of things, as we make objects. And you could then say that this is all reality, that thought is therefore also real.

K: Thought is real.

DB: And there is one part of reality influencing another part of reality.

K: Also, one part of illusion influences another part of illusion.

DB: Yes, but now we have to be careful because we can say there is that reality which is not made by man, by mankind. But that's still limited. The cosmos, for example, as seen by us is influenced by our own experience and therefore limited.

K: Quite.

DB: Any thing that we see, we see through our own experience, our own background. So that reality cannot possibly be totally independent of man.

K: No.

DB: It may be relatively independent. The tree is a reality that is relatively independent but it's our consciousness that abstracts the tree.

K: Are you saying that man's reality is the product of influence and conditioning?

DB: Yes, mutual interaction and reaction.

K: And all his illusions are also his product.

DB: Yes, they are all mixed together.

K: And what is the relationship of a sane, rational, healthy, whole man, to reality and to truth?

DB: Yes, we must consider that, but first may we look at this question of truth. I think the derivation of words is often very useful. The word *true* in Latin, which is *verus*, means 'that which is', the same as the English *was* and *were*, or German *wahr*. Now in English the root meaning of the word *true* is honest and faithful; you see, we can often say that a line is true, or that a machine is true. There was a story I once read about a thread that ran so true; it was using the image of a spinning wheel with the thread running straight.

K: Quite.

DB: And now we can say that our thought, or our consciousness, is true to 'that which is', if it is running straight, if the man is sane and healthy. And otherwise it is not, it is false. So the falseness of consciousness is not just wrong information, but is actually running crookedly as a reality.

K: So you're saying, as long as man is sane, healthy, whole, and rational, his thread is always straight.

DB: Yes, his consciousness is on a straight thread. Therefore, his reality...

K: ... is different from the reality of a man whose thread is crooked, who is irrational, who is neurotic.

DB: Very different. Perhaps the latter is even insane. You can see with insane people how different it is—they sometimes cannot even see the same reality at all.

K: And the sane, healthy, whole, holy man, what is his relationship to truth?

DB: If you accept the meaning of the word, if you say truth is that which is, as well as being true to that which is, then you have to say that he is all this.

K: So you would say the man who is sane, whole, is truth?

DB: He is truth, yes.

K: Such a man is truth. He may think certain things that would be reality, but he is truth. He can't think irrationally.

DB: Well, I wouldn't say quite that, I'd say that he can make a mistake.

K: Of course.

DB: But he doesn't persist in it. In other words, there is the man who has made a mistake and acknowledges it, changes it.

K: Yes, quite right.

DB: And there is also the man who has made a mistake but his mind is not straight and therefore he goes on with it. But we have to come back to the question: Does truth go beyond any particular man? Does it include other men, and nature as well?

K: It includes all that is.

DB: Yes, so the truth is one. But there are many different things in the field of reality. Each thing is conditioned, the whole field of reality is conditioned. But clearly, truth itself cannot be conditioned or dependent on things.

K: What then is the relationship to reality of the man who is truth?

DB: He sees all the things and, in doing this, he comprehends reality. What the word *comprehends* means is to hold it all together.

K: He doesn't separate reality. He says, 'I comprehend it, I hold it, I see it'.

DB: Yes, it's all one field of reality, himself and everything. But it has things in it that are conditioned and he comprehends the conditions.

K: And because he comprehends conditioning, he is free of conditioning.

DB: It seems clear then that all our knowledge, being based on thought, is actually a part of this one conditioned field of reality.

K: Now another question. Suppose I am a scholar; I'm full of such conditioned and conditioning knowledge. How am I to comprehend truth in the sense of holding it all together?

DB: I don't think you can comprehend truth.

K: Say I have studied all my life, I've devoted all my life to knowledge, which is reality.

DB: Yes, and it is also about a bigger reality.

K: And suppose you come along and say, 'Truth is somewhere else, it's not that'. I accept you, because you show it to me, and so I say, 'Please help me to move from here to that'. Because once I get *that*, I comprehend it. If I live *here*, then my comprehension is always fragmented. Therefore my knowledge tells me, 'This is reality but it is not truth'. And suppose you come along and say, 'No, it is not'. And I ask: Please tell me how to move from here to that.

DB: Well, we've just said we can't move ...

K: I'm putting it briefly. What am I to do?

DB: I think I have to see that this whole structure of knowledge is inevitably false, because my reality is twisted.

K: Would you say the content of my consciousness is knowledge?

DB: Yes.

K: How am I to empty that consciousness and yet retain knowledge that is not twisted—otherwise I can't function—and reach a state, or whatever it is, that will comprehend reality. I don't know if I'm making myself clear.

DB: Yes.

K: What I'm asking is: My human consciousness is its content, which is knowledge; it's a messy conglomeration of irrational knowledge and some that is correct. Can that consciousness comprehend, or bring into itself, truth?

DB: No, it can't.

K: Therefore, can this consciousness go to that truth? It can't either. Then what?

DB: There can be a perception of the falseness in this consciousness. This consciousness is false, in the sense that it does not run true. Because of the confused content it does not run true.

K: It's contradictory.

DB: It muddles things up.

K: Not, 'muddles things up'; it is a muddle.

DB: It is a muddle, yes, in the way it moves. Now then, one of the main points of the muddle is that when consciousness reflects on itself, the reflection has this character: It's as if there were a mirror and consciousness were looking at itself through the mirror and the mirror is reflecting consciousness as if it were not consciousness but an independent reality.

K: Yes.

DB: Now therefore, the action that consciousness takes is wrong, because it tries to improve the apparently independent reality, whereas in fact to do this is just a muddle. I would like to put it this way: The whole of consciousness is somehow an instrument that is connected to a deeper energy. And as long as consciousness is connected in that way, it maintains its state of wrong action.

K: Yes.

DB: So on seeing that this consciousness is reflecting itself wrongly as independent of thought, what is needed is somehow to disconnect the energy of consciousness. The whole of consciousness has to be disconnected, so it would, as it were, lie there without energy.

K: You're saying don't feed it. My consciousness is a muddle, it is confused, contradictory, and all the rest of it. And its very contradiction, its very muddle, gives it its own energy.

DB: Well, I would say that the energy is not actually coming from consciousness, but that as long as the energy is coming, consciousness keeps the muddle going.

K: From where does it come?

DB: We'd have to say that perhaps it comes from something deeper.

K: If it comes from something deeper, then we enter into the whole field of gods and outside agency and so on.

DB: No, I wouldn't say the energy comes from an outside agency. I would prefer to say it comes from me, in some sense.

K: Then the 'me' is this consciousness?

DB: Yes.

K: So the content is creating its own energy. Would you say that?

DB: In some sense it is, but the puzzle is that it seems impossible for this content to create its own energy. That would be saying that the content is able to create its own energy.

K: Actually, the content is creating its own energy. Look, I'm in contradiction and that very contradiction gives me vitality. I have opposing desires. When I have opposing desires I have energy, I fight. Therefore, that desire is creating the energy—not God, or something profounder—it is still desire. This is the trick that so many played. They say there is an outside agency, a deeper energy—but then one's back in the old field. But I realize that the energy of contradiction, the energy of desire, of will, of pursuit of pleasure is the content of my consciousness; that is, consciousness is creating its own energy. Reality is this; reality is creating its own energy. I may say, 'I derive my energy deep down', but it's still reality.

DB: Yes, suppose we accept that, but the point is that seeing the truth of this . . .

K: . . . that's what I want to get at. Is this energy different from the energy of truth?

DB: Yes.

K: It is different.

DB: But let's try to put it like this: Reality may have many levels of energy.

K: Yes.

DB: But a certain part of the energy has gone off the straight line. Let's say the brain feeds energy to all the thought processes. Now, if somehow the brain didn't feed energy to the thought process that is confused, then the thing might straighten out.

K: That's it. If this energy runs along the straight thread it is a reality without contradiction. It's an energy that is endless because it has no friction. Now is that energy different from the energy of truth?

DB: Yes. They are different, and as we once discussed, there must be a deeper common source.

K: I'm not sure. You are suggesting that they both spring out of the same root.

DB: That's what I suggest. But for the moment there is the energy of truth that can comprehend the reality and . . .

K: . . . the other way it cannot.

DB: No, it cannot; but there appears to be some connection in the sense that when truth comprehends reality, reality goes straight. So there appears to be a connection at least one way.

K: That's right, a one-way connection—truth loves this, this doesn't love truth.

DB: But once the connection has been made, then reality runs true and does not waste energy or make confusion.

K: You see, that's where meditation comes in. Generally, meditation is from here to there, with practice and all the rest of it. To move from this to that.

DB: Move from one reality to another.

K: That's right. Meditation is actually seeing what is. But generally meditation is taken as moving from one reality to another.

Saanen, 1 August 1975

WHAT IS THE action of a man who is not caught in time? What is the relationship between reality and truth, if there is such a thing as truth, and what is a man who lives in the world of reality all the time to do? Caught in that world of verbal, imaginative reality, the world of conclusions, ideologies, tyrannies, what is a human being to do? Shall we go into that? What is the difference, or what is the relationship, between truth and reality? We have said reality is all that thought has put together, all that thought reflects upon, all that thought remembers as knowledge, experience, and memory. Thought acts in that area, and lives in that area, and we call that reality.

We are saying that the root meaning of that word *reality* is *res*, thing. So we live with things, we live with things created by thought as ideas, we live with things called conclusions, which are all verbal, and we have various opinions, judgements, and so on. That is the world of reality. And what is the relationship between that and truth? How shall we find this out? This was one of the problems of the ancient Hindus, and of some philosophers and scientists, both ancient and modern: Is there such a thing as truth, and if there is, is it within the field of reality, or is it outside reality; and if it is outside, what is the relationship between that and reality?

What is the activity of reality? What takes place in the field of reality? Shall we begin with that, and see its meaning, its significance, and its value? And when we have completely understood the field of reality, then we can inquire into the other, not the other way round. Because one's mind may not be capable of inquiring into truth. But we *can* inquire into the world of reality, its activity, how destructive or constructive it is, and so on. When we are absolutely clear, logical, sane, and healthy about the world of reality then we can proceed to find out if there is truth. Not ask what truth is, because then we speculate about it, and our speculation is as good as somebody else's.

So what is activity in the world of reality, both outwardly and inwardly, psychologically? In that world of reality there is always duality, the 'me' and the 'you', we and they. This duality expresses, acts in the world of reality as nationalities, as religious divisions, as political division and tyrannies and domination; all this is actually going on. So there is this activity of duality—the 'me' and the 'you', and the 'me' separating itself from the actual, and having a conflict with the actual.

The world of reality is created by thought. Thought is movement in time and measure. That thought has created the centre; that centre separates itself from thought, and then that centre creates duality as the 'you', and the 'me'. Not verbally, not intellectually, but actually, does one see the reality of this? This is the truth; 'that which is' is the truth. And do I see 'that which is'? That is, thought creating a centre, that centre assuming power, domination, and creating division between the centre and the periphery. Thought, having created the centre, that centre not only becomes a cohesive, unitary process, but it also acts as a dividing thing. Do you see it as clearly as you see this tent? The tent is real, it has been created by thought; it is independent of thought but it is actual.

So we live outwardly and inwardly, psychologically, in the field of reality, which is basically not only fragmentary but divisive.

It is dual, divided. That is our life. One of the symptoms of this division is the centre trying to control thought, trying to control desire, trying to control various appetites, various reactions. So the centre becomes the factor of division. This is fairly simple. That is, conflict is always part of the field of reality. That conflict is not only within myself, but outward, in my relationship to others.

Conflict is one of the principles of reality, as division is one of the principles, and from that division conflict arises. This is factual. The centre separates itself from violence, and then that centre acts upon the violence, controlling it, dominating it, trying to change it into non-violence, and so on; from the centre there is always the effort made to control, to change. This is happening politically, in the democratic world as well as in the tyrannical world where the few dominate the many. The few are the centre—I don't know if you see the beauty of all this—and the few want unity, and therefore they must dominate.

So in the field of reality, division is one of the basic principles. That is, the centre trying to control thought. Let's stick to this and understand it. We try to control anger, we try to control various forms of desire, always from the centre—the centre being what thought has created that has become permanent, or rather attributed to itself the quality of permanency.

Q: You can do this in the privacy of thought.

K: If you are by yourself you can do this, but if you are with others you cannot live a life in which there is no control—is that it? I don't think you realize what you have said. That if you are by yourself perhaps you could do this, but if you have to live with others you cannot do this. Who are the others? We divide by thought as 'you' and 'me', but the actuality is, you are me, I am the world, and the world is me, the world is you. I wonder if you see this.

Q: That is not true.

K: I think it would be more correct if you used the word *incorrect* rather than say it is not true. Correct means care; it comes from the word *care*, accurate; accurate means care. You say, that is not so. Now let's look at it. Basically, whether you live in America, France, Russia, China, or India, we are the same—we have the same suffering, the same anxiety, the same grief, arrogance, uncertainty. Environmentally, culturally, we may have different structures and therefore act superficially differently, but fundamentally you are the same as the man across the border.

Q: I need privacy.

K: Oh, you still want privacy. Who is preventing you? I don't understand the question. If you say, 'I still want privacy', you mean you still want to be enclosed by a house, by a garden, by a wall round your house, or enclosed so as not to be hurt. So you say, 'I must have a wall around myself in order not to be hurt'.

As we were saying, in the field of reality, conflict and duality are the actual things that are going on—conflict between people, conflict between nations, conflict between ideals, conflict between beliefs, conflict between states, armaments—the whole field of reality is that. It is not an illusion, *maya*, as the Hindus would say. In Sanskrit *ma* means measure, so they say that in the field of reality there is always measurement, and therefore that is illusory because measurement is a matter of thought, measurement is a matter of time, from here to there, and so on. They said that is illusion. But the world they wanted is also an illusion created by thought.

So in the field of reality can one live completely without control? Not permissiveness, not doing what you want to do, because that is too childish. Because you can never do whatever you want to do. Is it possible to live a life without a shadow of conflict?

Q: It seems that when we are aware of all these processes that thought tries to control, this brings conflict and then to control thought brings more conflict. So why control?

K: No, sir, if I may go into it a little bit. Have you ever tried, or known how, to act without control? You have appetites—sexual, sensory appetites. To live with those appetites, not yielding to them, not suppressing them, nor controlling them, but see these appetites and end them as they arise? Have you ever played that—not 'played', have you ever done this?

Q: It's impossible.

K: No, sir, I'll show it to you. Don't say you can't do anything, the human mind can do anything. We have gone to the moon; before this century they said 'impossible', but we have gone to the moon. Technologically you can do anything, so why not psychologically? *Find out;* don't say, 'I can't, it's impossible'. Look, go into it step-by-step and you will see it. You see a beautiful house, a lovely garden, a desire arises, and how does this desire arise? What is the nature of desire? And how does it arise? I'll show it to you. There is visual perception of a house with a beautiful garden; it is architecturally beautiful, with nice proportions, lovely colours, and you see it. Then that vision is communicated to the brain; there is sensation; from sensation there is desire; and thought comes along and says, 'I must have it', or 'I can't have it'. I don't know if you have watched all this. So the beginning of desire is in the beginning of thought. Thought is physical as well as chemical. There is the perception of that house, sensation, contact if you touch it, and desire and thought. This happens, sexually, visually, psychologically, intellectually.

There is that beautiful house, the seeing, the sensation, the desire. Can that desire end, not move with thought as possessing and so on? The perception, sensation, desire, and the ending.

Not thought coming along and saying, 'I must'—in that there is no control. I am asking if you can live a life in the world of reality without control. All action comes from a desire, a motive, a purpose, an end. Surely this is simple, isn't it?

You eat a good, tasty omelette; what takes place? The brain registers the pleasure, and demands that pleasure be repeated tomorrow. But that omelette is never going to be the same. What we are trying to point out is: to taste and not let it register as a desire, as a memory, and end it.

Q: We are not quick enough to stop the thought.

K: Therefore learn. Let's learn *about it*, not *how to do it*. You see, one's mind, or brain, is traditional: You are always saying, 'I can't, tell me what to do'—that is the pattern of tradition. What we are saying is very simple: which is, the seeing, the sensation, and the desire. You can see the movement of this in yourself, can't you? When you see a beautiful car, a beautiful woman, or a beautiful man, or whatever, sensation arises, and desire. Now be alert to watch it, and you will see, as you watch it, that thought has no place.

I am suggesting that in the field of reality conflict is the very nature of that reality. So if there is an understanding, a radical change, in you, if there is the ending of conflict in a human being, then it affects the whole consciousness of man, because you are the world, and the world is you. Your consciousness with its content is the content of the world.

So we are asking: Can a human being live in the world of reality without conflict? Because if he cannot, then truth becomes an escape from reality. So he must understand the whole content of reality, how thought operates, what the nature of thought is.

The field of reality is all the things that thought has put together, consciously or unconsciously, and one of the major symptoms of that reality, a disease of that reality, is conflict—between individuals, between classes, between nations, between you and me. Conflict outwardly and inwardly is between the centre that thought has created and thought itself, because the centre thinks it is separate from thought. There is a conflict of duality between the centre and the thought; and from that arises the urge to control thought, to control desire.

Now is it possible to live a life in which there is no control? I am very careful in using that word *control*, which does not mean doing what you want, permissiveness, all the modern extravagances that have become vulgar, stupid, meaningless. We are using the word *control* in quite a different sense. One who would want to live in complete peace must understand this problem of control. Control is between the centre and thought—thought taking different forms, different objects, different movements. One of the factors of conflict is desire, and its fulfilment. Desire comes into being when there is perception and sensation. That's fairly simple and clear. Now can the mind be totally aware of that desire and end it, not give it movement first?

Q: There is no recording in the brain as memory, which then gives vitality and continuity to desire.

K: That's right. I don't know if you get this point. I see a beautiful picture and one response is to have it. Or I may not have that response, I may just look at it and walk off, but if there is a response to possess it, then that sensation as desire is registered in the brain and the brain then demands the possession of it and the enjoyment of it. Now can you look at that picture, see the desire, and end it? Please experiment, it is so simple once you understand the whole movement of it.

Q: Sir, I don't recognize that I have a desire until afterwards. In other words, there is no recorder in my mind that tells me I am having desire.

K: We said that conflict seems to be the nature of the world of reality. And we are trying to find out if it is possible to live without conflict. And we said conflict arises when there is duality, the 'me' and the 'you', and the centre created by thought and thought itself And the centre tries to control, to shape thought. Therein lies the whole problem of conflict. And desire arises through sensation—sensory perception. And sensory perception of objective things involving belief is illusion. I can believe that I am something when I am not; therefore, there is the problem of conflict. So is it possible to live a life totally without conflict? I do not know if you have ever put this question to yourself. Or do we live in the world of tradition and accept that world, that conflict, as inevitable?

Q: Sir, I am not conscious of living in conflict.

K: All right, then you say, 'I am not conscious that I live in conflict'. We are talking over together this question of reality and truth. That's how this began. We said that unless you understand the whole nature of reality with all its complexities, mere inquiry into what truth is is an escape. And we are saying let us look into the world of reality, the world of reality that thought—and nothing else—has created. In that world of reality, conflict is the movement of life. I may not be conscious of that conflict sitting here but unconsciously, deeply, there is conflict going on. This is simple enough.

Conflict takes many forms, which we call noble and ignoble. If a man has ideals and is trying to live up to those ideals—which is conflict—we call him marvellous, a very good human being. Those ideals are projected by thought. And the centre pursues that and so there is conflict between the ideal and the actual. This is what is happening in the world of tyranny, dictatorship. The few know what they think is right and it is for the rest to follow. So this goes on all the time. And it is the same with regard to authority—the authority of the doctor, the scientist, the mathematician, the informed man, and the uninformed man. The disciple wants to achieve what his guru has, but what the guru has is still in the world of reality. He may talk about truth but he is conducting himself in the world of reality, using the methods of reality, which is division between himself and the disciple. This is so obvious.

From Truth and Actuality, *Saanen, 25 July 1976*

Questioner: Is a motive necessary in business? What is the right motive in earning a livelihood?

Krishnamurti: What do you think is right livelihood? Not what is the most convenient, not what is the most profitable, enjoyable, or gainful; but what is right livelihood? Now, how will you find out what is right? The word *right* means correct, accurate. It cannot be accurate if you do something for profit or pleasure. This is a complex thing. Everything that thought has put together is reality. This tent in which we meet has been put together by thought; it is a reality. The tree has not been put together by thought; but it is a reality. Illusions are reality—the illusions that one has, imagination, all that is reality. And the action from those illusions is neurotic, which is also reality. So when you ask this question, 'What is right livelihood?', you must understand what reality is. Reality is not truth.

Now what is correct action in this reality? And how will you discover what is right in this reality?—discover for yourself, not be told. So we have to find out what accurate, correct, right action, or right livelihood is in the world of reality, and reality includes illusion. Don't escape, don't move away, belief is an illusion, and the activities of belief are neurotic; nationalism and all the rest of it are another form of reality, but an illusion. So taking all that as reality, what is the right action there?

Who is going to tell you? Nobody, obviously. But when you see reality without illusion, the very perception of that reality is your intelligence, isn't it, one in which there is no mixture of reality and illusion. So when there is observation of reality, the reality of the tree, the reality of the tent, reality that thought has put together, including visions and illusions, when you see all that reality, the very perception of that is your intelligence. So your intelligence tells you what you are going to do. Intelligence is to perceive what is and what is not—to perceive 'what is' and see the reality of 'what is', which means you don't have any psychological involvement, any psychological demands, which are all forms of illusion. To see all that is intelligence; and that intelligence will operate wherever you are. Therefore, it will tell you what to do.

Then what is truth? What is the link between reality and truth? The link is this intelligence that sees the totality of reality and therefore doesn't carry it over to truth. And the truth then operates on reality through intelligence.

Conversation at Brockwood Park, 28 June 1979

Walpola Rahula: I want to ask you one thing. We all talk of truth, absolute truth, ultimate truth; and seeing it and realizing it; we always talk about it. According to Buddha's teachings, these are very important central points, the essence really. And Buddha says clearly that there is only one truth, there is no second. But this is never defined in positive terms. This truth is also equated with nirvana. The terms *ultimate* or *absolute truth* are used as synonyms of nirvana.

Nirvana is never defined, except in mostly negative terms. If it is described in positive terms, it is mostly metaphorically, in a symbolic way. And as you know, there was the original, authentic teaching of the Buddha called the Theravada, the 'tradition of the elders'. Then about the first century B.C., the Mahayana, a later development, began to grow, as a free interpretation of the Buddha's teaching. And there is a very beautiful Mahayana text called the teaching of the Bodhisattva Vimalakirti. At a great gathering of Bodhisattvas and disciples in his house, the question was put: 'What is non-duality?' That is, non-duality is another word for the absolute truth, or nirvana. In Sanskrit it is called *advaya*.

Krishnamurti: Advaita, in Sanskrit, yes.

WR: No, *advaita* is different from *advaya*. In Buddhist terminology *advaya* means neither existence nor non-existence. The Buddha says, 'The world is duality', that means, either is or is not, either exists or does not exist, either is right or wrong, that is *advaya*, according to Buddhist teaching. The Buddha says the world depends on this. But the Buddha teaches without falling into this error. The question was, 'What is *advaya?*' And there are thirty-two definitions. So the assembly asks Vimalakirti for his opinion. And the sutra says, it is very interesting, that Vimalakirti answered the question with a thundering silence.

K: Quite.

WR: If you speak, it is not non-duality. When I gave a series of lectures, I was asked by a professor in Oxford, 'Can you formulate this non-duality or truth?' I said the moment you formulate, that is not non-duality; it becomes duality the moment you formulate it. So, just as they asked long ago, I ask you today: What is truth, what is absolute truth, what is ultimate truth, and what is that non-duality as you see it? Tell us. It is a challenge.

K: Do you think, sir, there is a difference between reality and truth? And is truth measurable by words? If we could distinguish between what is reality and what is truth, then perhaps we could penetrate more deeply into this question.

What is reality? The word *res* means thing. What is the thing? Could we say that everything that thought has created is reality—including the illusions, the gods, the various mantras, the rituals, the whole movement of thought, what it has brought about in the world, the cathedrals, the temples, the mosques, and their content? That is reality like the microphone—it is made by thought, it is there, actual. And nature is not created by thought.

It exists. But we human beings have used nature to produce things, like our houses, chairs, and so on. I mean, a beautiful cathedral, a beautiful poem, a lovely picture, are all the result of thought. So could we say then that anything that thought has created, brought about, put together, is reality?

Mary Zimbalist: When you speak of the beauty of the object, are you including its quality of beauty as reality, or the object itself, with beauty perhaps being some other quality? Are you including the idea of the beauty of that object in this category?

K: Yes, both. So could we do that, sir, say that reality, including the illusions it has created, as well as the material things it has created through technological knowledge and so on, could we say all that is reality?

WR: Yes. May I add a little to that? According to Buddhist thought, Buddha's teaching, there is relative truth or reality.

K: Don't let's use truth and reality, just . . .

WR: Yes, let us say reality. Reality is relative and absolute.

K: Of course.

WR: What you say is fully accepted, that is reality.

K: That is, everything that thought has created is reality. Dreams, all the sensory and sensuous responses, all the technological world, all the things that thought has put together as literature, poems, paintings, illusions, gods, symbols—all that is reality. Would you accept that?

Feroz Mehta: Yes, but the word *reality* has its denotation, its first meaning as well as its connotation. And through the centuries people have tended to talk of reality more in terms of one of its connotations of ultimate reality.

K: I know, but I would like to separate the two—truth and reality. Otherwise we mix our terms all the time.

FM: That is true.

Scott Forbes: Are you also including nature in reality?

K: No, that tree is not created by, thought. But out of that tree man can produce chairs and so on.

SF: Is there, then, a third category of things, which is neither truth nor reality? Or are you calling nature . . .

K: Nature is not created by thought. The tiger, the elephant, the deer, the gazelle—they are obviously not created by thought.

WR: That means you don't take the tree as a reality.

K: I take it as a reality, of course it's a reality, but it's not created by thought.

WR: That's true. Then are you saying that you include only things created by thought in reality?

K: Yes.

WR: Of course, that is your own definition.

K: No, I'm trying to be clear about our understanding of the two terms *truth* and *reality*.

WR: Yes, I understand, leave the word *truth* for another purpose.

K: Not another purpose, let us look at reality—what is reality? The world is reality.

WR: Yes.

K: These lamps are reality. You sitting there, this person sitting here, are realities. The illusions that one has are an actual reality.

MZ: But sir, the people sitting there are not created by thought.

K: No.

MZ: So could we more or less define another category for living creatures, nature, trees, animals, people?

K: A human being is not created by thought. But what he creates...

MZ: Yes. So the reality category of which you are speaking is man-made, in a sense.

K: Man-made. Like war is a reality. You're a bit hesitant about this.

FM: Could we regard all that is apprehended through the senses, and then interpreted by the brain, as reality?

K: That's right, sir.

SF: At one time we made a distinction, in talking, between reality, which was anything that was created by the mind, and actuality, which is anything that could be captured by the mind, anything that exists in time and space.

K: Yes.

SF: And then there is truth. Now, reality was part of actuality. In other words, the tree was an actuality, not a reality.

K: Why do you want to separate . . .

SF: Otherwise it becomes very confusing, because if we say, look, you and I, as people, are not created by thought, we're not reality.

K: You want to separate actuality, reality, and truth. Is that it?

SF: Well, I just offer that as a convenient definition of words that we used before.

K: Would we say that the actual is what is happening now?

FM: Yes, that's a good way of putting it. The point that arises there is: Are we capable of apprehending the totality of what is happening now? We apprehend only a portion of it.

K: Yes, but that's a different point, we can go into that. But what is happening is actual. That's all. Not whether we understand, comprehend the whole of it or part of it and so on. What is happening is the actual.

FM: Yes, that is the fact.

K: That is a fact. So, what do you say to all this, sirs?

WR: I am still hesitating, I'm waiting to see more.

K: Whether a mind can see the actual, incompletely or completely, that's not the point for the moment. The question is whether the mind can apprehend, perceive, observe, or see that from reality you cannot get to truth.

Stephen Smith: That's quite a big jump, probably.

K: Sir, could we put it this way too. As you pointed out, all the sensory responses are the beginning of thought. And thought, with all its complex movements, is what is happening now when we're talking. And what is happening is the actual, and the interpretation or the understanding of what is happening depends on thought. All that, including illusions and the whole business of it, is reality.

FM: Yes, that is so.

K: If we agree or accept that for the moment, then the question arises: Can the mind, which is the network of all the senses, actualities and so on, apprehend, see, observe what is truth?

FM: Provided the mind can be free of all its conditioning.

K: I'll come to that a little later. But that's the problem. To find out what absolute truth is, thought must be understood—the whole movement and the nature of thought must be gone into, observed. And so has its relative place, and therefore the mind becomes absolutely still and perhaps out of that, in that stillness, truth is perceived, which is not to be measured by words.

FM: Yes, there I'd agree completely.

WR: Yes, I agree with that.

K: Now, there are these two. A human being is caught in the movement of thought. And this movement projects what truth is.

FM: This is the mistake that man makes.

K: Of course. He projects from this to that, hoping to find what truth is. Or projects what he thinks is truth. And the truth can be put in different words—God, Brahman, as it is called in India, or nirvana or moksha, all that business. So our next question is: Can the mind cease to measure?

FM: That is to say, the mind as it functions at present in each one of us as an individual.

K: As human beings. Measurement is our whole educational, environmental, and social conditioning. Would you agree?

WR: Yes.

K: Then what is measurement?

FM: Limitation.

K: No, what is measurement, to measure? I measure a piece of cloth, or measure the height of the house, measure the distance from here to a certain place and so on. Measurement means comparison.

SS: Well, there's also psychological measurement in all this.

K: Yes, there is physical measurement and psychological measurement. One measures oneself, psychologically against somebody. And so there is this constant measurement of comparison, both externally and inwardly. I'm giving a lecture—what's the idea?

WR: Well, I put the question to you. As they put the question to Vimalakirti, I put the question to you.

K: What is the question?

WR: What is non-duality? What is truth?

K: As long as thought is measuring there must be duality.

WR: Absolutely, that is a fact, that is so.

K: Now, how has this conditioning come about? You understand, sir? Otherwise we can't move away from this to that. How has this constant measurement, comparison, imitation—you know, the whole movement of measurement, why has man been caught in it?

WR: All measurement is based on self.

K: Yes, but how has it come about? Why are human beings, wherever they live, conditioned through this measurement? One wants to find out what the source of this measurement is. You follow, sir?

SS: Part of it seems to be the fruit of observation, because you observe the duality of life in terms of night and day, man and woman, the change of seasons and this kind of thing, which is a certain kind of contrast, there's a certain apparent contrast. So it may seem a natural step to say that there is therefore a kind of contrast or comparison that is applicable in man's own life.

K: There's darkness and light, thunder and silence.

Parchure: It seems that thought needs a static point to measure, and itself is moving constantly. In a state of continuous flux or movement, it can't measure, so it creates a static point that is immovable, which is taken as the centre of the self. From there only you can measure.

K: Yes, sir. I mean, the very words *better, greater,* in the English language, are measurement. So the language itself is involved in measurement. Now, one needs to find out, doesn't one, what the source of this measurement is, why man has employed this as a means of living? One sees night and day, a high mountain and low valleys, a tall man, a short man, a woman, a man, a child, old age—physically there are all these states of measurement. There is also psychological measurement, that's what I'm talking about, much more than the mere physical movement of distance and so on. Why has man been held in this measurement?

SS: Probably he thinks it's the way forward to some extent, because, if you're a farmer and you plant a crop in a certain way, and you get a poor result, the next year you plant in a different way, and you get a better result.

K: Yes, so it is time. Go on, sir, a bit more.

SS: It includes the ability to reflect, to have experience, to reflect on experience, to produce something better out of that experience in terms of, probably, an established notion of what is the good, what is the better thing to have, or what is the right situation of things.

K: Of course, but I want to go a little further than that. Which is, why has man used time as a means of progress? I'm talking psychologically, not time that is necessary to learn a language, to develop a certain technology, and so on.

P: Perhaps the need for security of thought for itself.

K: No, time, which is measurement.

FM: Do you think that our tendency is, that starting with the facts, the physical facts of difference, in size, in quantity, and so forth, we apply that analogically to the psychological process?

K: Yes, that's what I want to get at. Or, without measurement, there would have been no technology.

FM: That's true.

Narayan: In science and mathematics, as they progress, measurement becomes more and more refined, and each refinement leads to a further step of progress, computers and so on. In one sense, measurement and refinement of measurement do lead to a certain kind of progress, in science and technology.

K: Of course.

WR: But we are not talking of physical measurement so much as psychological measurement.

K: Yes. Why has man used psychological time as a means of self-growth, self-aggrandizement? He calls it 'getting better', getting more noble, achieving enlightenment. All that implies time.

N: Is it, as Mehta says, carried over from the day-to-day living of measurement physically to the psychological field? Is it carried over, or does it exist in the psychological field without reference to this?

K: That's what we're discussing. Whether there is any psychological evolution at all.

SF: Could we say that we began to apply measurement to the psychological field, out of habit, because that's what we've been using for the physical field, but also could we have made that transfer because it's very comfortable to think that I might be in a mess now but later I'll be fine?

K: Of course, sir. Let's be clear on this. At the technological, physical level, we need time. We need time to acquire a language, time to build a house, time to go from here to there, or time for a developing technology or science; we need time there. So let's be clear on that. But I'm asking something else. Do we need time at all, psychologically?

WR: What is it that creates time?

K: Thought, thought is time.

N: So doesn't thought have something to do with it?

K: Which is what we're saying: time is movement. So thought is movement, time is movement from here to there; one is greedy, envious, I need time to be free of it. Physical distance and psychological distance. One is questioning whether that is not an illusion—not the physical distance but the psychological distance. To put it very succinctly, is there, psychologically, tomorrow?

FM: Only in terms of anticipation.

K: Ah, because thought says, I hope to.

FM: And in addition to thought, there is the fact of our physical experience, of day and night, and therefore the words *tomorrow* and *today*.

K: There is yesterday, today, and tomorrow; that is a reality, that is also a measurement. But we are asking, Is there psychological time at all, or has thought invented time, psychological time, in order to feel that it can achieve or live in some kind of security?

WR: What is time?

K: Time, sir, is movement

WR: Yes, time is nothing but the unbroken continuity of cause and effect. That is movement.

K: Movement, we said. Cause, effect, effect becomes the cause and so on.

WR: That is time. We give the word *time* to that movement.

K: Yes, which is movement. It's now five minutes past twelve, it's a movement till it reaches one o'clock. That's one aspect of time. And also the aspect of time that is from here, physical distance, to there. I have to go to London and it takes time to get there.

WR: Yes, that is another conception of time.

K: Another time. We are looking at the various facets of time.

WR: Yes, another time.

MZ: Sir, would you say that thought in itself implies time, because the action of the mind consulting thought, going through the thought process takes time, even if it's a very quick, short amount of time?

K: Surely, because thought is the response of memory, and memory is time. Let's stick to one thing, which is, there is physical time, yesterday, today, and tomorrow, time as movement.

FM: What we call chronological time.

K: Let's call that chronological time. Time also for distance. Time also for cause and effect—acorn and tree. To climb a mountain requires time. So we are saying, time, physically, exists. Physically, the baby grows into the man and so on. So time is necessary, time exists. That's an actuality, that is a reality. We are questioning whether, psychologically, there is time at all. Or thought has invented time as a means of either achieving security or it is too lazy to completely transform itself. So it says, 'Give me time'. Give me time to be strong psychologically. Psychologically give me time so that I get rid of my anger, my jealousy, or whatever it is, and I'll be free of it. So time is being used as a means of achieving something psychologically.

MZ: But then one must ask you about the use of the word *psychological* in this instance because if a thought process is involved and we just said time is implicit in thought, how can you be without thought psychologically?

K: We are coming to that.

MZ: Or is the psychological realm in this discussion outside of thought, or part of thought, or could it be either?

K: Isn't the whole psyche put together by thought?

SS: There seems to be a question here, whether it is or not.

K: I'm asking, sir, go slowly. Isn't the whole psyche the 'me'?

SS: Is that the psyche?

K: Isn't it? The 'me' is what I think, what I want, what I don't want, and so on; the whole self-centred movement of the 'me' is put together by thought.

MZ: If that is so, then how would it be possible for there not to be time involved in any psychological movement?

K: We're going to go into that. I want first to be clear that our questions are understood.

N: Would you make a distinction, sir, between hope and aspiration, because many people say to aspire is something noble, but to hope is . . .

K: Aspiring is time. Hoping is also time.

N: But in aspiration there seems to be the idea of something very right.

K: I aspire to become God—it's so silly.

N: In the whole religious world there is aspiration. Would you say that?

WR: Of course, in religious traditions there is always aspiration. What we are discussing, I think, is whether you can see truth without thinking or time, whether seeing truth is now, this moment, or whether you postpone it till you become better.

K: Ah, no.

WR: That is the question.

K: That is, the moment you introduce the word *better* . . .

WR: That is what I am saying. Truth is something you see now.

K: No, we haven't come to truth yet. I am very careful, sir; I don't want to enter the world of truth yet. One wants to be clear whether one's thinking is logical, sane, and rational, or comes to a conclusion that is illusory. So one wants to examine the whole nature of time, psychologically. That's all I'm talking about. If there is no tomorrow psychologically, our whole action is different. But, psychologically, we say, tomorrow is important. Tomorrow I will do this, tomorrow I hope to change, psychologically. I'm questioning that, because all our aspirations, hope, everything, are based on the future, which is time.

N: You would say then that any aspiration, however noble, is in the field of reality.

K: In the field of thought, yes.

FM: Yes, because it is a formulation.

K: A formulation by thought.

FM: Exactly. So would I be right in saying you are concerned with being free of the time factor totally, in psychological terms?

K: Yes, sir. Otherwise I am caught, our mind is living always in a circle.

FM: Yes, that is true. We are tied to the past, to that which has become fossilized.

K: Yes, the past modifying the present and going off into the future. This past modifying itself into the future is time. So when one says, 'I will be better', 'I will understand', or 'I will try', all these are involved in time. So I question that, whether it's merely an invention of thought for its own—whatever reason—and so it is illusory, and so there is no tomorrow.

FM: In psychological terms.

K: Of course, we said that very clearly. If one is envious, envy is a sensory response, and therefore thought has created this envy. Now, generally we say, give me time to be free of that envy.

FM: Yes, provided we perceive that this is envy.

K: Oh, yes, I'm envious, you've a bigger house, you're better dressed, you've more money, all the rest of it, everybody perceives this envy, this jealousy, this antagonism. So is it possible, being envious, to be free of it instantly, and not allow time to intervene? That is the whole point.

FM: Isn't the envy the psychical reaction to what is perceived through the senses?

K: Yes, that's right.

FM: And are not the sense functionings . . .

K: . . . actual.

FM: Yes, they are. Determined by actual physical conditions?

K: Yes, obviously.

FM: So psychical reaction follows the sensuous activity. And that involves the pleasure/pain drive within us.

K: Obviously. One sees you driving in a big car. And I'm driving a small car, so there is comparison.

FM: Yes, the comparison arises, surely, partially through what others have put before us, that this is better than that. This is more pleasant or this is less pleasant. So we get into the psychological habit.

K: That begins from childhood. You are not as good as your brother in examinations, and the whole education system is based on this comparative evaluation of one's capacities. Now we're going, you see, we're moving away from . . .

WR: Yes.

SS: Yes, sir, didn't we just come to the fact that anything that is involved in measurement and thought cannot get rid of measurement and thought?

K: First it must realize the actuality of it. Not say, 'Yes, I've understood it'.

SF: Does it realize that with thought?

K: No.

SF: So then what is the . . .

K: Wait, we're coming to that slowly. Do we see that we've used time psychologically and that psychological usage of time is an illusion? First I want to see, we must be clear on that point. I will reach heaven, I will become enlightened, I will eventually, through various series of lives, or one life, achieve nirvana, moksha, all this. All that is psychological time. We are questioning whether that thing is an illusion. It is an illusion if it is part of thought.

SF: Right. Now we can't, we don't use thought in order to see all this.

K: No, wait. Do we understand even verbally?

SF: Even with thought?

K: With thought. Communication now is, between us, through words. Those words have been accumulated and so on, and for the moment we both of us speak in English, we understand the meaning. Now, do we see—see not through argument, through explanation, through rationalization, that thought has created this psychological time as a means of achieving something?

MZ: Can we see that still within the thought process, still within the realm of thought?

K: Now, wait.

MZ: Is that the seeing you're talking about?

K: No, I'm coming to that. I'm coming to that slowly, I want to lead up to it, otherwise it won't be clear. Am I all right, are we following each other, sir, or not?

WR: I am following.

K: Is this accurate, sir?

K: That I can't yet say. Because I don't know where we are going.

K: I don't know where I'm going either! But this is a fact.

WR: Yes, that's right. That is, I am watching.

N: I think there's also some difficulty in apprehending what you're saying, because there is maturity and growth in nature through time.

K: We've been through that, Narayan, don't go back to it.

N: I'm not going back to it, but unconsciously you're identified with it. Is there maturity and growth in human beings through time? There is some kind of maturity through time.

K: We said that.

N: Yes, so one gets stuck to that.

K: One holds on, is attached to this idea of time as self-improvement, not only physically but psychologically.

N: I don't even say *self-improvement*, but maturity. A kind of natural growth, comparing yourself with nature, as you see everywhere.

K: Yes, but wait, what do you mean by maturity? We may have different meanings for that word *mature*. A tree is mature at a certain age, a human being physically is mature at a certain age. And mature cheese!

N: Yes, the whole, the fruit from the bud.

K: Yes, the fruit is matured to be picked. And so on. But is there psychological maturity at all? That's my whole point.

P: Perhaps there is a factor of life, intellectual maturity, which is at the mental level.

MZ: Within the illusory world, psychologically there is a certain maturity, but it's still founded on thought and time.

K: Yes, but I'm just asking, Maria, do we understand clearly, even verbally, and so intellectually, that we have used time as a psychological catalyst to bring about change? Right? And I'm questioning that catalyst.

FM: May I inquire, sir, when you say, 'Do we see that psychological time is an illusion?', what precisely do you mean by the word *see?*

K: I mean by that word *see*, observe without the interference of thought.

FM: That means, to be completely conscious, to be completely aware of time being an illusion as a fact.

K: Yes, to see this as I see a snake, and not mistake it for a rope.

FM: No. Would you agree that that involves a complete transformation of your mode of awareness, your consciousness? When you're really conscious of something, you don't have to . . .

K: Now, wait a minute. Again, sir, the words *consciousness* and *conscious* . . .

FM: Those are difficult words.

K: Those are difficult words. I see this—can I see this and not call it a microphone? Not call it anything, but see the shape, just observe without any reflection?

FM: Quite, without naming it.

K: Naming and all the rest of it, analysing.

FM: In other words, to see is a whole seeing, almost in the sense of your being what you see.

K: No, no. That becomes then a duality, you become that. No.

FM: You don't become that in the sense that you are merged into it. But you are awake in terms of a unitary whole.

K: Just a minute, sir. These again are rather difficult words.

WR: I don't think that is what he means.

K: Sir, to observe implies—first, let's look at it as it is generally understood—to observe a tree, I name it. I like it or don't like it, and so on. But what we mean by observation, by seeing, is to listen first and not make an abstraction of it into an idea, and so the idea sees. I wonder if you see?

WR: Yes, yes.

K: Say, for instance, I said a little earlier that psychologically there is no time, psychological time is the invention of thought, and may be an illusion. Now to listen to that without interpreting it, thinking what do you mean, rationalizing it, or saying, 'I don't understand', 'I do understand', just to listen to that statement and not make an idea of it, but just to listen. As one listens in that way, in the same way observe, see. What do you say, sir?

WR: I want to ask you, what you are trying to tell us?

K: I'm trying to say, sir, that truth cannot possibly be perceived, be seen, through time.

WR: Right.

K: Wait a minute, you can't agree.

WR: Not agree, I see it. That is why I was waiting to ask you what you are trying to say.

K: I'm trying to say that—I'm not trying, I'm saying!

WR: Yes, of course, what you want to say.

K: Sorry. I'm saying that man, through comparison with the outer world, has created psychological time as a means of achieving a desired, rewarding end.

WR: I agree.

K: No, do you see that as a fact—a fact in the sense that it is so?

SF: Is the facility of the mind that sees that the same facility that sees truth?

K: Look, Scott, first you listen, don't you, to that statement?

SF: Yes.

K: How do you listen to that statement?

SF: Well, at first I just listen.

K: You listen. Do you make an idea about it?

SF: Often, later, yes.

K: No, it's a simultaneous process going on. You listen and you get an idea of it and the idea is not the actual observation. That's all I'm saying.

SF: But if there is that . . .

K: No, sir, from Greeks and the Hindus, our whole structure is based on ideas. And we are saying idea is not actual happening, which is the actual listening.

FM: The idea is just a picture of the actual listening.

K: Yes, which is an evasion, an avoidance of actual observation.

FM: Of the immediate fact.

K: Yes, looking or listening.

SS: Then there may be something that we are evading constantly.

WR: Yes.

SS: I would like to suggest, as we've been talking about thought and the various things that it has devised in order to create some kind of freedom or liberation or salvation or redemption, that there may be some driving factor that is part of thought, or there may be a driving factor that accounts for this, which may be sorrow.

K: Yes, sir, escape from pain through reward.

SS: It seems to apply to the most sophisticated and the more primitive civilizations, all of them.

K: Obviously. Because all our thinking is based on these two principles, reward and punishment. Our reward is enlightenment, God, nirvana or whatever you like to call it, away from anxiety, guilt, all the pain of existence; you know, the misery of it all.

FM: Is it not possible to be free from the idea of reward or punishment?

K: That's what I'm saying. As long as our minds are thinking in terms of reward and punishment, that is time.

FM: How is it that our minds think that way?

K: Because we're educated that way.

FM: Yes, true.

K: We are conditioned from childhood, from the time of the Greeks in the West, because for them measurement was important, otherwise you couldn't have all this technological knowledge.

FM: And would you say that this is due to the fact that we are tied to the idea of a separate 'me', a separate 'I'? Supposing one sees, hears, touches, etc., all in terms of a wholeness, an awareness of wholeness?

K: One can't be aware of the wholeness unless one has understood the movement of thought, because thought is in itself limited.

FM: Thought, yes, of course, which means the intrusion of the self-consciousness as a separate something. Otherwise it won't be there.

K: Sir, how did this self-separative consciousness come into being?

FM: Conditioning in the first instance.

K: It's so obvious.

FM: I, you, me.

K: Of course, measurement.

FM: Measurement, exactly. And that inevitably gets transferred analogically to the realm of the psyche, the realm of the mind . . .

K: Of course.

FM: . . . or whatever it is.

K: So we come to this point. You make a statement that psychological time has been used by man as a means of achieving his reward. It's so obvious. And that reward is away from the pain that he's had. So we are saying that this search for reward, or the achievement of the reward, is a movement of time. And is there such a thing at all? We have invented it, it may be illusion. And from this illusion I can't get to reality—I mean to truth. So the mind must be totally, completely free of this movement of measurement. Is that possible?

FM: As a short answer, I would simply say yes.

K: Yes. Either you say yes as a logical conclusion, or a speculative assertion, or a desire, or a concept, or it is so.

FM: Yes, an *of-courseness* is there. If there is a sense of *of-courseness*, of course it is so, then there is . . .

K: Then I assume it is so, but I go on the rest of my life moving in the other direction.

FM: If one really sees . . .

K: Ah, that's what we are saying.

FM: . . . then one doesn't go in the other direction.

K: So that's what we're saying, do we see it, or is it that we *think* we see it?

FM: Quite.

MZ: Can we go back for a moment? You said you observe, you hear the statement, you observe it. Actually, what does the mind do in that observation?

K: Please, if I can put it this way: Please don't accept what one is saying, but let's find out. Observation in the sense of a seeing without naming, without measuring, without a motive, without an end. Obviously that is actually seeing. The word *idea* from the Greek, the word itself, means to observe.

MZ: But, sir, we would probably all agree with that. And what is acting at that moment? It is a kind of logic, I think, in most people.

K: No.

MZ: What you've said seems very evident.

K: Observation implies silence and not forming any conclusion, just to observe silently, without any psychological or sensory response except either visual or inward, insight without the responses of memory.

WR: Without any value judgement.

K: Yes.

FM: Would you say, sir, that implies without any reaction from the brain or the senses?

K: Yes, sir, that. Wait, it's a dangerous thing to bring in the brain. Because then we have to go into the whole question of the brain and I don't want to do that for the moment. It implies though that thought is absolutely quiet in observation.

FM: Scientists, for example, who have really new, remarkable inspirations, or again, great artists when they create wonderful things—this happens when everything is quiet inside, which allows this new to emerge, the new, the truly new, the pulse of creation.

K: Yes, sir, but that insight is partial. The scientist's insight or perception is partial.

FM: Partial, yes. That is to say, the formulation of that insight.

K: Ah, his insight is not only a formulation but there is the very fact of his insight, because insight implies a whole transformation of his daily life; it isn't just, I'm a scientist and I have an insight into mathematics, into matter, into the atom. Insight implies the way the man lives as a whole.

WR: That is perfectly so.

FM: And any insight is a particular manifestation rooted in the background of the whole.

K: Ah, no, we go off into something there. I won't accept—sorry, not that I won't accept it, but it's rather confusing. Sir, let us talk a little bit about insight or seeing. Insight implies an observation in which there is no remembrance of things past, therefore the mind is alert, free from all impediments and so on, just to observe. Only then you have an insight. But that insight we are talking about involves his whole life, not as a scientist, or as an artist. They have partial insight.

WR: That is only a small fragment.

K: A fragment of insight, but that's not what we're talking about. So it comes to this.

WR: What we are talking of is the whole of existence.

K: Of course, man's existence.

FM: So in that state of observation that you're talking of, there is no reaction whatsoever.

K: Of course, obviously. It isn't cause/effect reaction.

FM: Quite, it's free of causality.

K: Of course, obviously, otherwise we are back to the old cause being a motive and so on.

WR: And that seeing is beyond time. It is beyond time, that seeing is not limited or caught in time.

K: And that insight is not involved in time.

WR: That's right. And naturally it is neither cause nor effect.

K: Yes. But, wait a minute. Have we got this insight into this psychological invention of time by thought as achieving some result? Have you got insight, do you see it, or it is just at a verbal, ideological level?

WR: Or whether it is a fact that psychological time is necessary for seeing.

K: No, sir. We went into this question. Man has invented time, psychologically, to achieve a desired end, a purpose, a reward. Does one see this as an idea, or it is so? It's so obvious it is so. Then how is man—this is the point—how is man, a human being, to totally move away from that, totally transform this whole concept of idea, of time? I say it's only possible when you have an insight into this whole thing, which doesn't involve effort, which doesn't involve concentration, all that. This is real meditation.

FM: In fact, it just happens.

K: It's real meditation.

WR: Indeed.

SF: Sir, there is a dilemma that I think many people find themselves in when they listen to that, which is that in order to have this insight . . .

K: Ah, you can't *have* it.

SF: Well, in order for this insight to occur, there must be an insight into thought. And it seems like it's somewhat of a closed circle.

K: No. Thought, as we said, is the response of memory, and memory is knowledge, experience, and so thought is moving from the past, always from the past, it is never free from the past.

SF: And we said that there must be a seeing, an observing without . . .

K: Seeing that.

SF: Right. Now we can't see that with thought. We were saying that there must be a seeing, an observing, which is an insight . . .

K: . . . into thought.

SF: . . . into thought.

K: Wait, just hold it. Now, thought is the response of memory. Memory, stored in the brain through experience, has become knowledge. So knowledge is always the past. And from that thought arises. This is irrefutable, I mean, this is so.

SF: Yes.

K: Now is this an idea or an actuality that you yourself have perceived? Do you yourself see that the ascent of man through knowledge is not so? Man can only ascend perhaps technologically, but psychologically, if he continues with the accumulation of knowledge, he's caught in the trap. Do you see that? Or do you make it into an idea and say, 'What do you mean by it?' and so on.

SF: But, sir, just to see that, I must be free.

K: No, observe, you first listen.

SF: Yes.

K: Listen without analysis, without interpretation, without like or dislike, just listen. And if you so listen you have absorbed it, absorbed the fact that thought is the response of memory. Then you can proceed. Then can thought ever free itself from its mother, from its roots, from its source? Obviously not.

SS: But thought can be aware of its own activity.

K: Of course. We went through all that.

MZ: Would you say that if insight comes into being at that moment, then that insight doesn't fall back into the thought mechanism?

K: Oh, no, of course not. Say, for instance, you have an insight and you act. Now let's be clear. Insight means instant action, not have an insight and act later. That very insight implies action and you act. That action is always right, right being accurate, precise, without any regret, without any effort, without any reward or punishment, it is so.

SS: That action is not necessarily doing anything, though. It may be non-action in terms of doing things externally.

K: You may have to, both externally and inwardly. If I have an insight into attachment, attachment to ideas, attachment to conclusions, attachment to persons, attachment to my knowledge, experience—if I have an insight into that, the whole thing is abandoned.

WR: And may I put it, sir, in another way—I don't know whether you agree—to see this illusion, to see this illusion.

K: Yes, but one must be sure that it is an illusion.

WR: Whether you call it illusion or whatever name you give to it, to see . . .

K: 'What is'. That's all.

WR: Yes, see 'what is'. Don't give it a term.

K: No, to see 'what is'.

WR: To see 'what is' is to see the truth.

K: No, no, you see, you're bringing in truth—I'm not yet ready for that.

WR: I want to get to it before one o'clock! I don't want to postpone it, but your main thesis is don't put in time.

K: Yes, I said that, just now.

WR: Yes, to see 'what is', as it is, is to see the truth. That's what I would like to put in, to cut it short. And truth is not away from . . .

K: Sir, I don't know what it is.

WR: That is what I am saying, to see.

K: I don't know what it means to see. You have told me what it means to see, but I may not see. I may think I see.

WR: Yes, then you are not seeing.

K: I must be very clear that I am not *thinking* I'm seeing.

WR: No.

K: Sir, my whole life is that—I 'think' I see.

WR: Which is different from seeing.

K: You say so, but ordinary persons say, I see, yes. Which is, I think I see what you're saying. But I may not see actually 'what is'. I *think* I see 'what is'.

SF: This might be a simple question, but you say that the ordinary person says, 'I see what you're saying', but in fact he doesn't. It's just mentally or intellectually that he sees something. Could we say what is going to bring about for the ordinary person this correct seeing, this seeing without thought?

K: I explained it, sir. First I must listen. But *do* we listen, or do we have all kinds of conclusions, our minds so filled with them that they aren't capable of listening? You see me, you say, 'He's an Indian, what the heck, get rid of him, he knows nothing'. Or you say, 'Well, he's considered to be so and so, this or that'. So you don't actually listen.

SF: Well, then the question is—I would just change the terminology—what could bring about that correct listening?

K: It has been said, through suffering, which is nonsense. It has been said, make effort, which is nonsense. You listen when somebody says, 'I love you', don't you? So can you do the same thing, listen to what you think is unpleasant?
    So, sir, now come back to this question of truth. Do we have a discussion this afternoon? Can we then pursue truth?

WR: No, I don't want to wait for truth! (laughter)

K: You want it all in five minutes, sir?

WR: Not even five minutes.

K: One minute?

WR: One minute. If you can't do it in one minute, you can't do it in five hours.

K: I quite agree. All right, sir, in one second. Truth is not perceivable through time. Truth doesn't exist when the self is there. Truth doesn't come into existence if thought is moving in any direction. Truth is something that cannot be measured. And without love, without compassion, with its own intelligence, truth cannot be.

WR: Yes, now again you have given it in negative terms, in the real tradition of the Buddha.

K: You have translated into terms of tradition, therefore you've moved away from the actual listening to this.

WR: I listened, I listened very well.

K: Then you've captured the perfume of it.

WR: Yes, and I have captured the perfume of what you said. And that is why I wanted to have it in one minute.

K: So, sir, what, then, is the relationship of truth to reality? Be careful. I mean, are these two everlastingly divided?

WR: No.

K: No, no.

WR: No, I don't hesitate, I am not hesitating. They are not divided.

K: How do you know?

WR: I know it.

K: No, sir. 'They are not divided'. Now what do you mean by that, sir?

WR: That is what I said, to see.

K: No, just a minute, sir. Truth and reality, you say, are not divided. That means thought and truth are always together. If they are not divided, if something is not divorced, separated, it is together, a unitary movement. Thought . . .

WR: Not thought.

K: Wait, reality, that's why I went into it, sir. Reality is everything that thought has put together. We are all agreed that this is so. We may use the terminology, the word *reality*, as something else, I don't care, but for the present we are saying, reality is all the things that thought has put together, including illusion. And truth is nothing whatsoever to do with this, it can't be. And therefore the two cannot be together.

WR: To see that illusion, or whatever it may be, to see 'what is', is to see the truth. 'What is' is the truth. There is no truth apart from that. 'What is' is the truth, what is not is untrue.

K: No, sir, no. We said reality is the movement of thought. Right, sir? And truth is timeless. Truth is timeless, it's not your truth, my truth, his truth—it is something beyond time. Thought is of time, the two cannot run together, that's what I'm saying.

WR: What I said is that there are not two. That is again duality, again you are dividing.

K: No, I'm not. I'm pointing out, sir, I may be mistaken, but I'm just pointing out that thought has created such illusion, and has brought about so much deception, and it may deceive itself by saying, 'Yes, I've seen the truth'. Therefore I must be very clear, there must be clarity, that there is no deception whatsoever. And I'm saying that deception exists, will inevitably exist, if I don't understand the nature of reality.

WR: I think here we have come to truth. I don't know whether you . . .

K: I haven't come to truth, I can't go to truth.

WR: No, you see the truth.

K: I don't see the truth. There's a tremendous difference. I can't go to truth, I can't see truth. Truth can exist only, can be only, or is only, when the self is not.

WR: That is right.

Ojai, California, 8 May 1980

Questioner: There is a prevalent assumption these days that everything is relative, a matter of personal opinion, that there is no such thing as truth or fact independent of personal perception. What is an intelligent response to this belief?

Krishnamurti: Is it that we are all so personal that what I see, what you see, is the only truth? That my opinion and your opinion are the only facts we have? That is what the question implies: that everything is relative; goodness is relative, evil is relative, love is relative. If everything is relative, that is, not the whole complete truth, then our actions, our affections, our personal relationships are relative, they can be ended whenever we like, whenever they do not please us.

Is there such a thing as truth apart from personal belief, apart from personal opinion? Is there such a thing as truth? This question was asked in the ancient days by the Greeks, by the Hindus, and by the Buddhists. It is one of the strange facts in the Eastern religions that doubt was encouraged—to doubt, to question—and in religion in the West it is rather put down, it is called heresy.

One must find out for oneself, apart from personal opinions, perceptions, experiences, which are always relative, whether there is a perception, a, seeing, which is absolute truth, not relative. How is one going to find out? If one says that personal opinions and perceptions are relative, then there is no such thing as absolute truth; all is relative. Accordingly, our behaviour, our conduct, our way of life, is relative, casual, not complete, not whole, fragmentary.

How would one find out if there is such a thing as absolute truth, which is complete, which is never changing in the climate of personal opinions? How does one's mind, the intellect, thought, find out? One is inquiring into something that demands a great deal of investigation, an action in daily life, a putting aside of that which is false—that is the only way to proceed.

If one has an illusion, a fantasy, an image, a romantic concept, of truth or love, then that is the very barrier that prevents one from moving further. Can one honestly investigate what an illusion is? How does illusion come into being? What is the root of it? Does it not mean playing with something that is not actual?

The actual is that which is happening, whether it is what may be called good, bad, or indifferent; it is that which is actually taking place. When one is incapable of facing that which is actually taking place in oneself, one creates illusions to escape from it. If one is unwilling or afraid to face what is actually going on, that very avoidance creates illusion, a fantasy, a romantic movement, away from that which is. That word, *illusion*, implies the moving away from that which is.

Can one avoid this movement, this escape, from actuality? What is the actual? The actual is that which is happening, including the responses, the ideas, the beliefs and opinions one has. To face them is not to create illusion.

Illusions can take place only when there is a movement away from the fact, from that which is happening, from that which actually is. In understanding that which is, it is not one's personal opinion that judges but the actual observation. One cannot observe what is actually going on if one's belief or conditioning qualifies the observation; then it is the avoidance of the understanding of that which is.

If one could look at what is actually taking place, then there would be complete avoidance of any form of illusion. Can one do this? Can one actually observe one's dependency; either dependency on a person, on a belief, on an ideal, or on some experience that has given one a great deal of excitement? That dependence inevitably creates illusion.

So a mind that is no longer creating illusion, that has no hypotheses, that has no hallucinations, that does not want to grasp an experience of that which is called truth, has now brought order into itself. It has order. There is no confusion brought about by illusions, by delusions, hallucinations; the mind has lost its capacity to create illusions. Then what is truth? The astrophysicists, the scientists, are using thought to investigate the material world around them, they are going beyond physics, but always moving outwards. But if one starts inwards one sees that the 'me' is also matter. And thought is matter. If one can go inwards, moving from fact to fact, then one begins to discover that which is beyond matter. Then, if one goes through with it, there is such a thing as absolute truth.

Bombay, 3 February 1985

WE ARE GOING to talk over together, if you will, what a holistic way of life is. The word *whole* means complete, not broken up into fragments, fragments as a businessman, an artist, a poet, a religious cuckoo, and so on, which is how we have divided our lives. You belong to a special group, with garlands and strange dress, and another group wears some other kind of costume. We are constantly categorizing, putting people into some drawer, so that they are this or that—Communists, Socialists, capitalists, and so on. So our life, if you observe closely, is broken up, fragmented. And why are we human beings, who have lived on this marvellous earth for a million years or 50,000 years, like this?

One of the main causes of this breaking up into pieces is that the brain is a slave to thought—thought being limited. Wherever there is limitation, there must be fragmentation. When I am concerned with myself—with my progress, my fulfilment, my happiness, my problems—I've broken down the whole structure of humanity to *me*. So one of the factors why human beings are fragmented is thought.

Also, one of the factors is time. Have you ever considered what time is? According to scientists, who are concerned with time, it is a series of movements. So movement is time. Time is not only measured by the watch, chronologically. Time is the sun rising, the sun setting; time is dawn and snow on the mountains and in the deep valleys, the darkness of a night and the brightness of a morning. And also there is psychological time, inward time. I am this, I will become that. I don't know mathematics, but one day I will learn all about it. That requires time. To learn a new language requires a great deal of time: three months, six months, or two years. That is also time. There is time to learn, to memorize, to have a skill, and there is also time as the self-centred entity saying, 'I will become something else'. So the becoming, psychologically, implies time also.

We are inquiring therefore into what time is? Not only the time to learn a skill, but also the time that we have developed as a process of achievement: 'I don't know how to meditate. I'll sit cross-legged, and one day I will learn how to control my thought. One day I will achieve what meditation is supposed to be'. So I practise, practise, practise. Then I become a mechanical monkey. Because whatever you practise, you become mechanical in doing. Time is the past, the present, and the future. Time is the past, all the experiences, knowledge that human beings have achieved that remains in the brain as memory. That's simple. And that past is operating now in the present. All the memories, all the knowledge, all the experiences, the tendencies, and so on are the background, and that background is operating now. So you are the past. And the future is what you are now, perhaps modified, but the future is the past modified. The past modified in the present is the future.

Your tradition as a cultural country for the last three to five thousand years, this vast accumulation of knowledge, culture, all the things human beings have been struggling with, inquiring into, having a dialogue about—all that is smashed in the present, because the economic conditions demand it. The past is broken up, modified, and is going to be the future. This is a fact. So if there is no radical change in the present, tomorrow you will be the same as you are today. So the future is now. The future—not the future of acquiring knowledge, but the psychological future—is that the psyche, the 'me', the self, is the past memory, and that memory modifies itself now and goes on. So the future and the past are in the present. So all time—past, present, and future—is contained in the now. It's not complicated. It's logical. So if the human brain doesn't change now, instantly, the future will be what you are, what you have been.

Is it possible to change radically, fundamentally, now, not in the future? It is very simple, this. Don't complicate it. We are the past. There is no question about it. And that past gets modified in reaction, in challenges, in various ways. And that becomes the future. Look, you have had a civilization in this country for three to five thousand years. That is the past. And modern circumstances demand that you break away from the past. And you have no culture anymore now. You may talk about past culture, enjoy the past fame, and the past long centuries, but all that is blown up, scattered by the present demands, by the present challenge. And that challenge, that demand, is changing into an economic entity. So the past being challenged by the now becomes the future.

Also, we want roots, identification—identification with a group, with a family, with some guru, and that is why you put on these strange garments. I know you won't go away from that, but that's your job. So we want to be identified with a group, with a family, with a nation, and so on. And the threat of war is a major factor in our life, because war may destroy our roots psychologically; therefore, we are willing to kill others. And also we want to be identified. You understand? Identified with a name, identified with a family, and so on. So these are the major factors of our fragmented lives. Now do you listen to the truth of it or do you listen merely to a description of what is being said and carry the description, not the truth of it? The idea of it and not the fact of it.

Say, for instance, the speaker says, 'All time is now'. If you understand that, it is the most marvellous truth. Now, do you listen to it as a series of words and therefore as a sound, a word, an idea, an abstraction of the truth as an idea, or do you capture the truth of it, not make an abstraction of the truth? Which are you doing? Living with the fact, or making an abstraction of the fact into an idea and then pursuing the idea, not the fact? That is what the intellect does. Intellect is necessary. Probably we have very little intellect anyhow because we have given ourselves over to somebody. Intellect implies and demands reason, logic, and seeing things very, very clearly, to discern. Also, the capacity of the intellect is to gather information and act upon that information. And when you hear a statement like 'All time is now' or 'You are the whole of humanity, because your consciousness is one with all the others', how do you listen to those statements Do you make an abstraction of them as an idea? Or do you listen to the truth, to the fact of it; the depth of it, the sense of immensity involved in that? Ideas are not immense. But a fact has tremendous possibility.

So a holistic life is not possible when the cause is thought, time, and the desire for identification and roots. These prevent a way of living that is whole, complete. Now when you hear this statement, your question will be, 'How shall I stop thinking?' A natural question isn't it? 'How shall I?' I know time is necessary to learn a skill, a language, a technological subject, and so on. Time is necessary for research. But I've just begun to realize that the becoming from 'what is' to 'what should be' involves time and may be totally wrong. It may not be true. So you begin to question, or do you say, 'Well, I don't understand what you are talking about, but I will go along with it'? Which is actually what is taking place.

I wish we would be very honest with ourselves. Honesty is one of the most important things, like humility. Humility cultivated by a vain man is part of vanity. Humility has nothing to do with vanity, with pride. It is a state of mind—a brain that says, 'I don't know, but let me inquire'. Never saying, 'I know'. So now, you have listened to the fact that all time is now—the fact. You may not agree or you may agree. That is one of our dreadful things, agreeing and disagreeing. Why should we agree or disagree? It is a fact that the sun rises in the east, that's a fact. You don't agree or disagree. The sun has set. It is a fact. So can we both look at facts? So there is no division between those who agree and those who don't agree. There is only seeing things as they are. You can say, 'I don't see', then that's a different matter. Then we can go into why you don't see, and so on. But when we enter into the area of agreement and disagreement, then we become more and more confused.

So the speaker has said our lives are fragmented. That's a fact. Our ways of thinking are fragmented. You are a businessman, earn lots of money and then you go and build a temple or give to charity. See the contradiction. And we are never honest to ourselves—deeply honest. Not honest in order to be something else or to understand something else, but to be unquestionably clear, to have an absolute sense of honesty, which means no illusions. If you tell a lie, you tell a lie and you know it and say, 'I've told a lie'. Not covering it up. When you are angry, you are angry. You say you're angry. Don't find causes and explanations for it or how to get rid of it. This is absolutely necessary if you are going to inquire into much deeper things as we are doing now. Not make a fact into an idea but remain with the fact. That requires very clear perception.

Now, having said all this we say, 'Yes, I logically, intellectually, understand this'. That's what you would say. And, 'How am I to relate to action what I have logically, intellectually understood, what I have heard? What is the truth?' So you've already created a division between the intellectual understanding and action. Do you see this? So listen, just listen. Don't do anything about it. Don't say, 'How am I to get something? How am I to put an end to thought and time?'—which you can't, which would be absurd because you are the result of thought and time. So you go round and round in circles. But if you listen, not react, not say, 'How?', but actually listen, to some lovely music, the call of a bird, listen, that 'time is all in the now'. And thought is a movement, so thought and time are always together. They are not two separate movements, but one constant movement. That's a fact. Listen to it.

Then there is identification: You want to be identified, because in identification as a Hindu, a Muslim, a Christian, or whatever it is, you feel secure. That's a fact. And identification is one of the causes of fragmentation in our lives, like time, thought, and also wanting security and therefore taking roots in a particular country, a particular family, community, a group. Listen, don't do anything—these are the factors of our fragmentation. Now, if you listen to it very carefully, that very listening creates its own energy. Do you understand? If I listen to the fact of what has been said, and there is no reaction because I'm just listening to it, then that implies gathering all my energy to listen. That means giving tremendous attention to listening. And that very listening breaks down the factors of, or the causation of, fragmentation. If you do something then you're acting upon the fact. But if there is only observation, without distortion, without prejudice, that observation, that perception, which is great attention, that very attention then burns away the sense of time, thought.

Bombay, 7 February 1985

Questioner: Sir, I want to have a clarification. You said just now: a true or a false statement. What is true and what is false?

Krishnamurti: Truth? What is a true statement or a false statement? How are you going to find out? From another? What is a false statement? And what do you mean by false? Take a very ordinary example: Many people accept that nationalism is a marvellous fact, that we must be nationalistic. Is that a false statement or a true statement? How do you look at it? How do you find out? Say, for instance, most of you believe in God. Don't you? All right. You believe in God. Is it a false statement or a true statement? How do you find out? You can believe in anything you like, in any illusion, in any fanciful, romantic, sentimental concept. And belief may not necessarily be true. No belief is. So how do you find out these things?

How do you find out if there is God? To find out you must have a free mind, not a believing mind. You must have a mind that is capable of investigating, looking, doubting, questioning—of not being afraid. Fear can create that which is false as true, and that which is true as false. This is what is happening in the world. So to find out what is true, what is truth, there must be a great sensitivity, a sense of freedom—not just the idea of freedom but actual freedom, freedom from fear, and so on. Most of us have many illusions, and those illusions have become truth, real. And to be free of illusion is the most necessary and arduous work. Be totally free of all illusions; then only can you find out what is true and what is false.

Bombay, 9 February 1985

OUR CONSCIOUSNESS IS shared, one with all humanity. We don't see the beauty, the immensity of this. We go back to our own pattern, thinking we are all individuals, fighting, striving, competitive, each wanting to fulfil his own beastly little self. Because it means nothing to us, we go back to our old way of life. So it is much better not to listen to all this. If you listen to truth and you don't act upon it, it acts as poison. That's why our lives are so shoddy and superficial.

We must talk over together why man has not only lived in disorder for thousands and thousands of years, but also why man is perpetually seeking pleasure: pleasure in possessions, in achievement, in power, in having status, not only sexual pleasure, which is maintained by constantly thinking about sex, imaginary pictures, making images. That is, thought gives pleasure, sensation is turned into pleasure.

So we must understand what pleasure is, why we seek pleasure. We are not saying it is right or wrong. We are not condemning pleasure, nor are we condemning desire. Desire is part of pleasure. The fulfilment of desire is the nature of pleasure. So we ought to talk over together not only the nature of pleasure, but also what desire is. Desire may be the cause of disorder, each one wanting to fulfil, achieve, his own particular desire. We are concerned with serious matters, not with entertainment, not with intellectual games, but with our lives, our daily monotonous, boring, trivial, shoddy lives.

So together we are going to investigate if desire is one of the major causes of disorder. Desire, in its fulfilment, in its achievement, in any direction, gives pleasure, gratifies. So we ought together to investigate, explore, what desire is. Not condemning it, not escaping from it, not, as most religions have said, trying to suppress it, which is absurd. So let us look at it. What is desire? Probably most of us have not thought about it at all. We have accepted it as a way of life, that it is a natural instinct of man or woman, and we say why bother about it. Except those people who say they have renounced the world—which they never have done—those who enter monasteries where they try to sublimate desire with worship of a person, of a symbol, and so on. Please bear in mind that we are not condemning it. We are trying to find out together what desire is, why man has, for a million years, not only physically, biologically, but also psychologically, been caught in the trap of desire, in the network of desire. Will you investigate with the speaker, or just listen to the speaker, while he investigates, explores on his own?

How easy it is to be caught in explanations, in descriptions, and we are satisfied with commentaries, descriptions, and explanations. But we are not doing that. We have to explain, to describe, to point out, to put it in the framework of words. Desire is one of the most complex things to understand, not intellectually, but profoundly. I will explain, I will go into it, but you have to go into it too, not just agree or disagree, that's silly. We have to find out the nature of desire, how it is put together, what its origin, its beginning, is. Every animal on this earth has desire.

Every human being is caught in this network of desires and feels unhappy when his desires are not fulfilled, whether they be ideological, religious, platonic, or merely physical. What is the origin, the beginning, of desire? The speaker will describe, not analyse. There is a difference between analysis and perception. Analysis implies the analyser and the thing he is going to analyse, which means the analyser is different from the analysed. Are they different? Suppose I am the analyser and I am envious, and I begin to analyse why I am envious, as though I am different from envy. But envy is me. Envy is not separate from me. Greed, competition, comparison, all that is me. So we are not analysing. But we are looking, hearing, and, in the process, learning. Learning is not merely accumulating memory. That is necessary, but learning is something entirely different, it is not an accumulative process. You are moving, never recording, fresh.

Together we are observing what desire is, what the origin of desire is, why human beings are caught in it endlessly. If you have a little money, you want more money; if you have a little power, you want more power. And power in any form, whether over your wife or your children, politically, religiously, is an abominable, evil thing, because it has nothing to do with truth. We will go into that.

So what is the origin of desire? We live by sensation. If there were no sensation, both biologically and psychologically, we would be dead human beings. We live by sensation. The sound of that crow calling is acting on the eardrum, the nerves; and the noise is translated into the cry of a crow. That is a sensation. And sensation is brought about by hearing, or seeing, then contact. You see a nice garden, beautifully kept. It is green, rich, perfect, there are no weeds in it. A lawn that has been kept going for four hundred years is a lovely thing to see. First the seeing, then if you are sensitive you go and touch the grass. Seeing, contact, then sensation. Seeing a lovely garden, a nice car, a nice tree, and a beautiful man or woman. We live by sensation. It is necessary. If you are not sensitive, if you are dull, you are only half-alive—as most of us are.

So there is sensation, then what takes place? Take a very simple example: You see a nice sari, or a shirt in the shop. You see it, you go inside, touch it, and there is the sensation of touching it. You say, 'By Jove, what lovely material that is'. Then what takes place? There is seeing, contact, sensation; then what takes place after that? Are you waiting for me to tell you? If you see this for yourself, not being told by another, then you will become the teacher *and* the disciple. But if you repeat, repeat, repeat what somebody has said, including the speaker, then you remain mediocre, thoughtless, repetitive. So let's go into it.

There is seeing, contact, sensation. You see one of the latest cars from Europe, you touch the polish, the shape of it, the texture, then out of that there is sensation. Then thought comes and says how nice it would be if I got that. How nice it would be if I got into it and drove off. So what has happened? Thought has given shape to sensation. Thought has given to sensation the image of you sitting in that car driving off. At that moment when thought creates the image of you sitting in the car, at that second, desire is born. Desire is born when thought gives shape to sensation, gives an image to sensation.

Now the question is: Sensation is the way of existence, it is part of existence to be sensitive. And we have learned to suppress, or to conquer, or to live with desire with all its problems. Now if one understands, not intellectually but actually, that thought gives shape through the image, that at that second the origin of desire is there, then the question arises: Is it possible to see the car, touch it, but not let thought create the image, and so keep a gap?

One must find out also what discipline is. So let's talk about discipline and we will come back to desire afterwards. The word *discipline* comes from the word *disciple*. The etymological origin of that word is one who is learning, a disciple who is learning from his master. Learning, not conforming, not controlling, not suppressing, following, becoming obedient. On the contrary: learning from observation. That is, you are learning what desire is, learning about it, which is not memorizing.

Most of us are trained to discipline according to a pattern: copy, follow, obey. That's what you are all doing, hoping that discipline will bring about order. But if one is learning, then that very learning becomes its own order. You don't have order imposed by law or anything else.

So at the second that thought gives shape to sensation by giving it an image, desire is born. Can you learn, find out, whether it is possible to keep them apart to allow sensation to flower and not let thought interfere with it? You have never done all this. Then you will find out that desire has its right place. When you understand the nature of desire there is no conflict about it.

We ought also to talk over together what love is and sorrow and death. Shall we go on? This affects your daily life, it is not something you play with intellectually. It concerns your life, not somebody else's life, the way you live. After all these million years, look what our lives are, how empty, shallow, violent, brutal, inconsiderate, thoughtless. Look at it. All this has created such havoc in the world. We all want to have high positions, achieve something, become something. Looking at all this, there is great sorrow, isn't there? Doesn't every human being in the world, whether highly placed, or an uneducated villager, go through great sorrow? He may recognize the nature and the beauty and the strength of sorrow, but he goes through pain like you do, and mankind has gone through sorrow for a million years. We haven't solved the problem. We want to escape from it. We want it organized.

And what is the relationship of sorrow to love and death? Can there be an end to sorrow? This has been one of the questions mankind has asked for a million years. Is there an end to all the pain, the anxieties, the grief of sorrow? Sorrow is not only your own particular sorrow, there is the sorrow of mankind. Historically speaking, there have been five thousand years of war, every year there has been somebody killing somebody else, for their tribe, for their religion, for their nation, for their community, for their individual protection, and so on and so on. Have you ever realized this, what the wars have done? There is conflict over the Muslim, the Pakistani, and the Hindu. Have you ever gone into the question of wars that have created havoc, how many millions have cried? How many millions are being wounded, without arms, without legs, without eyes, even without a face?

So is there an end to sorrow and all the pain therein? And what is sorrow? Don't you know sorrow? Are you ashamed to acknowledge it? When your son or daughter, or somebody whom you think you love, is taken away, don't you shed tears? Don't you feel terribly lonely? You have lost a companion forever. We are not talking about death. But this immense thing that man goes through and never has a solution, an answer, for. Without ending sorrow there is no love. Sorrow is part of our self-interest, it is part of our egotistic self-centred activity. I cry for another—for my son, brother, mother. Why? Because I have lost something that I am attached to, I have lost something that gave me companionship, comfort, and all the rest of it. And with the ending of that person I realize how utterly empty or how lonely my life is. And then I cry. And there are many, many thousands of people ready to comfort me. And I slip very easily into that network, into that trap of comfort. Whether it is the comfort of a God, that is, an image put together by thought, or the comfort of some illusory concept or idea, it gives me comfort, and that's all I care about.

One needs to have a comfortable bed, a comfortable chair, but what is the urge, the desire for comfort psychologically, inwardly? We never question if there is any such comfort at all. Is it an illusion that has become our truth? An illusion can become our truth. Where there is illusion that there is God, that God has been created by thought, by fear. If you have no fear there is no God. But God has been invented by man through fear, through loneliness, through despair, through wanting this everlasting comfort. So we never question if there is comfort at all, which is deep abiding satisfaction. We all want to be satisfied, not only with the food that we eat, but also sexually, or by achieving some position of authority and therefore having comfort in that position. You know all this.

We must ask if there is any comfort at all. Is there anything that will be gratifying, satisfying, from the moment we are born until we die? Don't listen to me, find out. Give your energy, your thought, your blood, your heart, to find out. And if there is no illusion, is there any comfort? If there is no fear, do you want comfort? Comfort is another form of pleasure. Yes, this is a very complex problem of our life. While we are so shallow, empty, filled by other people's knowledge, by books, we are not independent human beings, free to find out why we are slaves. This is not a rhetorical question, it is a question that each one of us must ask. In the very asking and the doubting there comes freedom. And without freedom there is no sense of truth.

From Last Talks at Saanen 1985, *Saanen*, *21 July 1985*

So WHAT IS truth? Is there such a thing as truth? Is there such a thing—an absolute, irrevocable truth, not dependent on time, environment, tradition, knowledge, what the Buddha said, or what somebody said? The word is not the truth. The symbol is not the truth. The person is not the truth. Therefore there is no personal worship. K is not important at all. So we are seeking what is truth. If there is any. And whether there is something that is beyond time. The ending of all time. And they have said that meditation is necessary to come upon this. To have a quiet mind. We will go into that.

What is meditation? According to the dictionary, the word means to ponder over, to think over. Also it has a different meaning, both in Sanskrit and in Latin, which is to measure—which means, of course, comparison. There is no measurement without comparison. So can the brain be free of measurement? Not measurement by the ruler, by the yardstick, in kilometres, miles, but can the brain be free of all measurement, of becoming, not becoming, comparing, not comparing? Can the brain be free of this system of measurement? I need to measure to get a suit made. I need measurement to go from here to another place; distance is measurement, time is measurement. So can the brain be free of measurement, that is, of comparison, and have no comparison whatsoever so that the brain is totally free? This is real meditation. Is that possible living in the modern world with all the noise, the vulgarity, the circus that is going on in the name of religion, making money, having sex, breeding children? Can one be free of all that? Not in order to get something; to be free.

So meditation is not conscious meditation. It is not collective meditation, group meditation, solitary meditation, according to Zen, Buddhist, and Hindu systems. Meditation can't be a system because then you practise, practise, practise, and your brain gets more and more dull, more and more mechanical. So is there a meditation that has no direction, which is not conscious, deliberate? Find out.

That requires great energy, attention, passion. Then that very passion, energy, the intensity of it, is silence. Not contrived silence. It's the immense silence in which time and space are not. Then there is that which is unnameable, which is holy, eternal.

From Last Talks at Saanen 1985, Saanen, 25 July 1985

Questioner: How can our limited brain grasp the unlimited, which is beauty, love, and truth? What is the ground of compassion and intelligence? Can it really come upon each one of us?

Krishnamurti: How can our limited brain grasp the unlimited? It cannot, because it *is* limited. Can we grasp the significance, the depth of the quality of the brain and recognize the fact, the fact and not the idea, that our brains are limited by knowledge, by specialities, by particular disciplines, by belonging to groups, by nationalism, which is camouflaged, hidden, self-interest? The limitation comes into being essentially when there is self-interest. When I am concerned with my own happiness, with my own fulfilment, with my own success, that very self-interest limits the quality of the brain and the energy of the brain.

The speaker is not a specialist in the brain, though he has talked to several professional people about it. But the brain is the brain, not just their brains, but yours and mine. That brain has evolved through millions of years, in time and thought. It has evolved. Evolution means a whole series of events in time. It has taken two and a half million years, more or less. To put all the religious rituals together needs time. So the brain has been conditioned, limited by its own volition, seeking its own security, keeping to its own backyard, saying, 'I believe, I don't believe, I agree, I don't agree, this is my opinion, this is my judgement'—by self-interest. Whether it is in the hierarchy of religion or among the politicians, or in the man who seeks power through money, or the professor with his tremendous scholastic knowledge, or all the gurus who are talking about goodness and peace, it is part of self-interest. Face all this.

So our brain has become very, very, very small—not in its shape or size, but we have reduced the quality, the immense capacity, of it. It has improved technology, and also it has immense capacity to go inwardly, very, very deeply, but self-interest limits it.

To discover for oneself where self-interest is hidden is very subtle. It may hide behind an illusion, in neuroticism, in make-believe. Uncover every stone, every blade of grass to find out. Either you take time to find out, which again becomes a bondage, or you see the thing, grasp it, have an insight into it instantly. When you have a complete insight it covers the whole field.

So the questioner says, how can the conditioned brain grasp the unlimited, which is beauty, love, and truth? What is the ground of compassion and intelligence, and can it come upon each one of us? Are you inviting compassion? Are you inviting intelligence? Are you inviting beauty, love, and truth? Are you trying to grasp it? I am asking you. Are you trying to grasp the quality of intelligence, compassion, the immense sense of beauty, the perfume of love and that truth which has no path to it? Is that what you are grasping? Wanting to find out the ground upon which it dwells? Can the limited brain grasp this? You cannot possibly grasp it, hold it. You can do all kinds of meditation, fast, torture yourself, become terribly austere, having one suit, or one robe. All this has been done. The rich cannot come to the truth, neither the poor. Nor the people who have taken a vow of celibacy, of silence, of austerity. All that is determined by thought, all put together sequentially *in order to*. This is all the cultivation of deliberate thought, of deliberate intent. As someone said to the speaker, 'Give me twelve years and I'll make you see God'.

So as the brain is limited, do whatever you will, sit cross-legged in the lotus posture, go off into a trance, meditate, stand on your head or on one leg—whatever you do, you will never come upon it. Compassion doesn't come to it.

Therefore, one must understand what love is. Love is not sensation. Love is not pleasure, desire, fulfilment. Love is not jealousy, hatred. Love has sympathy, generosity, and tact, and so on. But these qualities are not love. To understand that, to come to that, requires a great sense and appreciation of beauty. Not the beauty of a woman or a man, or a cinema star. Beauty is not in the mountain, in the skies, in the valleys, or in the flowing river. *Beauty exists where the self is not.* You can see a great old tree, see the majesty of that tree, and say, 'How marvellous!' but the self hides behind that tree. So beauty exists only where there is love. And beauty, love, is compassion. There is no ground for compassion, it doesn't stay at your convenience. That beauty, love, truth, is the highest form of intelligence. When there is that intelligence there is action, clarity, a tremendous sense of dignity. It is something unimaginable. And that which is not to be imagined, the unlimited, cannot be put into words. It can be described: Philosophers have described it, but the philosophers who have described are not that which they have described.

So to come upon this great sense there must be the absence of the me, the ego, egocentric activity, the becoming. There must be the great silence in one. Silence means emptiness of everything. In that there is vast space. Where there is vast space there is immense energy, not self-interested energy, but unlimited energy.

Brockwood Park, 29 August 1985

Krishnamurti: [reading out a question] 'K says there is no path to truth'. Do you accept that? 'Is the faculty to see this outside myself? My consciousness and means of perception are entirely within me. How can I go without any means or tools towards the unknown goal? What will give me the need, the energy, to move in this direction?' There are so many things in this question.

First of all, the answer is not outside the question. The answer is not outside the problem. The answer is in the problem, in the question. We are always trying to find a satisfactory answer that is convenient, happy, pleasurable, and so on, outside the problem. Can we put aside all escaping from the problem, and look at the question together. 'K says there is no path to truth'. Why do you believe him? Why do you accept it? Why do you repeat it? 'K says'. Who is K to say it? What right has he? Or is it a reaction? You understand? As long as there are human beings, they have different opinions. So it may not be true. Let's first find that out.

There are the various Christian paths, the Catholic, the Protestant, and the innumerable divisions of Protestantism. And there is the Buddhist path, several paths according to the Buddha, though one never really knows what the Buddha actually said, or what Christ said. Then there are the Tibetan Buddhist paths. So there are the Christian, the Buddhist, and the Muslim paths, with their divisions. There are spread out before you all these paths to truth, whatever that may mean, to God, to illumination, to enlightenment, and so on; there are dozens of them. How will you choose? How will you choose the right path? Please tell me.

Audience: You have to know yourself.

K: Somebody says you have to know yourself. So why bother about paths? Why bother about truth? Why bother about what K says? Why don't you know about yourself? And how will you know about yourself? In what manner? How will you look at yourself as you would look at yourself in a mirror? It is easy to say look at yourself. Socrates and the ancient Greeks and before them the ancient Israelites, and before them the ancient Egyptians and the ancient Hindus, have all said in different ways, 'Know yourself'. And there are these paths in front of us. And we all want to achieve truth, whatever that is. And all these paths lead to that. That means truth is fixed. It must be, otherwise there would be no path to it. It must be stationary, it must have no movement, it must be dead, then there can be paths to it. [laughter] No, don't laugh, this is what we do.

So somebody like K comes along and says, look, don't bother about paths, it may be as though you are on a ship without a rudder and you find out, move, learn, keep on going. Not become stationary and make truth something permanent. And we want something permanent. Like permanent relationship. I am attached to my husband, wife, I want it to be permanent. We don't admit any change. And we are changing all the time, both biologically and psychologically, but I want to remain with something that is completely satisfactory, permanent, enduring, giving me security. And as I find there is really no security, then I have truth as the permanent entity towards which I am going. And there are all the gurus and the priests, who help you to go there.

So the questioner asks: What are the tools necessary to reach truth, which is pathless? The moment you have tools you have already created the path. Do you see this? The moment I have a means to do that, to achieve that, the means then becomes the tool and I have already got the truth towards which I am working. So the moment you have a tool, a means, a system, then you know what truth is; therefore, there is no point in having a tool. Do we see this? Or is this too illogical? Or too dastardly reasonable? The means is the end, the means is not different from the end.

You say, 'My consciousness and means of perception are entirely within me'. What do you mean by the word *consciousness?* It is fun if you go into all this. Not only to understand one's own brain capacity, but also to delve. You dig very deeply to find oil, go through all that trouble, and we won't even spend a second doing this in ourselves, for ourselves. So what do we mean by that word *consciousness?* Is that consciousness different from the 'you', from the 'me'?

What do you mean by consciousness? Books have been written about it by experts. And we are not experts. God forbid! We are just inquiring together, like two friends. What do you mean by consciousness? Everything that you are, isn't it? Your consciousness is made up of all its content: anger, jealousy, faith, belief, anxiety, aspiration, all the innumerable experiences that one has had, all the accumulation of all the little things of life, and also suffering, pain, insecurity, confusion, and the desire to escape from all this, and find something enduring. In it also is the fear of death, and inquiring what there is beyond. All that, this vast bundle, is our consciousness. We *are* our consciousness. And the content of consciousness makes up the whole entirety of consciousness, whether it is higher consciousness, lower consciousness, or the desire to expand consciousness, it is still within the field of consciousness. And that consciousness is me. There is no 'me' without that. When you say the 'me' is different, my consciousness is different, then you have a battle with it, struggle, conflict, all that ensues.

Our question then is: Is it possible first to discover for ourselves the content, to see the content? That is fairly easy—the way you comb your hair, the habits of speech, of thought. It is fairly simple to observe those, and also to become aware of one's own conditioning as British, as French, as Russian, and so on. It is also fairly easy to see our various religious inclinations—Catholic, Protestant, Hindu, Buddhist, following something or other—that is fairly easy. But to go beyond that, we don't need an Aqua-Lung, but we have to go very deeply, and to go very deeply one must understand the superficial thing first, and whether it is possible to be free from influence that conditions us. Is it possible?

Find out. Work at it. Put your tremendous energy into it, you have got tremendous energy, you don't want more. It took you a lot of energy to come here. If one may respectfully point out, use some of that energy to go into this. When you want something you go after it. That means one must not be indolent, one has to be a little active. And there is nobody to help you, no tool, no instrument, no leader, nothing to help you. You must really become helpless to find the real thing. I don't know if you understand that. If you are helpless, actually helpless, that means there is no help whatsoever from anybody, any book, any person, any environment. When you are in that state of real helplessness, then something else takes place. Then you begin to see things.

The questioner asks: What will give me the need, the energy, to move in the direction of truth. 'The direction of truth' means it is already over there [laughter]. I am not laughing. I am not disrespectful or cynical, but it is like that; when we use words like *direction* it is already *there*, it is already preconceived, already existing *there* because of your conviction or somebody told you and so on. Truth is really a pathless land. And that can only exist when fear and all the rest are not.

Q: I am afraid to change. If I change, what will happen afterwards? I am paralysed by this. Can you talk about this problem?

K: Delighted! I am afraid to change. If I change what will happen afterwards? I am paralysed by this. Why is one afraid of change? What do you mean by that word *change?* One has lived in this house across the lawn for nearly twenty years. One becomes attached to that particular room, to the nice furniture up there. One becomes attached. That means what you are attached to is what you are. If one is attached to that good old furniture, you are that furniture. So we are afraid to change. I am attached to that room. But fortunately the speaker travels a great deal.

So what does that word imply? Change from 'what is' to 'what should be', right? That is one change. Or change according to my old pattern but remain within the pattern, going across one corner of the field. I say I have moved, have changed, but it is still within the same, barricaded, barbwired field. Going north, east, west, south is change. Why do we use that word? Biologically one is told there is constant change in the blood, constant movement, one cell dies, another cell takes it place, a series of molecules, and so on. There is this constant change going on physically. And we are afraid to change. Could we drop that word *change?* Change implies time—doesn't it? I am this, I will change to that. Or I have been that and some event will come along, take place, and that event will change me, and so on. Change implies a movement in time, right?

So if we could drop those words *change* or *revolution* or *mutation*, all of which the speaker has used, then we are faced only with 'what is'. Not 'what should be'. Only face 'what is'. I am angry. That is 'what is'. I am violent. That is 'what is'. But to become politically or religiously non-violent is a change. To become non-violent when I am violent takes time. In that interval I am sowing the seeds of violence. That is all so simple.

So I remain with violence, do not try to change it. I am angry. That is a fact. There are no excuses for anger. I can find a dozen excuses for hate and anger, but inquiring into why I get angry is another escape from anger. Because I have moved away. So the brain remains with 'what is'. Then see what happens. That is, I am jealous of you. Not me personally. I am jealous of you because you look so much nicer, cleaner, have good taste, have a good brain. I am envious of you. Out of that envy comes hate.

Envy is part of hate. Envy is part of comparison. I would like to be like you but I can't be. So I become rather antagonized, I feel violent about you. So I remain with 'what is'. That is, I see I am envious. There it is, I am envious. That envy is not different from me. Envy is me. So I can't do anything about it. I hold it. I stay with it. Will you stay with it? Not escape, not find out the cause, or the reason, or go beyond it. I am envy. And see what takes place. First there is no conflict; obviously, if I am envious I am envious. Conflict only exists when I don't want to be envious.

So if I stay with it I have tremendous energy. Energy is like light focused on something that then becomes very clear. And that which is very clear you are not afraid of, paralysed by. It is so. I hope you understand.

What is important in this is not to escape, not to make an effort, but just to remain with 'what is'. If I am British, I remain with that. See what happens. How narrow it becomes. Sorry if you are British, forgive me—or French or Russian, or whatever it is. The thing itself begins to show its whole content.

Q: How does one meet aggression and psychological attack from a close relative from whom one cannot escape? [laughter]

K: How does one meet aggression and psychological attack from a close relative from whom one cannot escape? Are we all like that? I can't escape from my guru because I have committed myself to him or her and I have given up all my money to him. Don't laugh, this is taking place now.

What does it mean to be attacked psychologically, inwardly? When you are with a close friend or relative, there is always pressure psychologically, inwardly, going on between you. You know all this, I don't have to tell you. Always trying to do something about the other, attacking subtly, physically, or through innuendo, through subtle words, gestures, you are always trying to push the other into a certain pattern. Now the questioner says, What is one to do? I am living with you in the same house and you are bombarding me, I am bombarding you, not only with words and gestures but even a look, a feeling of irritation, and so on. What will you do not to be wounded, not to be pushed around psychologically? You may depend on that person financially. You may depend on that person for various psychological reasons. And the moment you depend you become a slave. The moment you are attached you are a goner! Don't look at somebody else, but let's look at ourselves.

If I am attached to you as the audience then I'm lost. Then I depend on you for my satisfaction, comfort, reputation, for my physical well-being, too. But if I don't depend on you, I have to find out why I don't depend on you. That means not only on you, I don't depend on anything. I want to find out if it's true. I may not show it to my close relative. I want to find out for myself whether it is possible, living in the same room, same house, with husband, wife, relative, and so on, to be totally impregnable. Not build a wall around oneself, that is fairly simple. I can build a wall around myself and say sorry and be polite about it, soft about it, and very affectionate, but it is still a wall. That means limitation. So is it possible for me to live vulnerably, and yet not be wounded? To be highly sensitive, not to be in any way responding according to my attachment? Go on, think it out. And if one is dependent on another financially, that becomes rather dangerous. Most of us are in this position.

If I am dependent financially on you, what happens between us? You then have the whip hand. Not only financially, but go further into it. Is it possible to live with another on whom I am financially dependent and know I am dependent because I can't do anything else? I can't start a new career. If I am quite young I probably could, but if I am fifty, sixty, or even seventy or ninety, then I can't start a new career. So then what shall I do?

So where do I draw the line of dependency? Psychologically I won't depend. For myself I won't depend on anybody, or on anything, or on any past experience. There is no dependence. But if one is dependent financially where do I draw the line? I have to put up with it because I can't start a new game. So how deep is that line? Is it just superficial? Or has the line great depth? So what is important in this question, if one understands it rightly, is freedom. Freedom is absolutely necessary. I depend on the milkman, on the supermarket, the postman, and so on, but otherwise, psychologically, I don't depend. I must be very clear on this.

Q: Some people seem to pick parts of what you say that fit their problems or interest and then discard the rest. What do you say to this?

K: What do I say to this? I don't have to say anything about it. What do *you* say? We are dealing together with the whole of life, not just part of it. The psychological world is immense, not just physical reactions and nervous responses, and memories and so on. That is part of the psychological structure, but it goes much deeper than that. We are dealing not only with the psychological world but with the violence that exists in the world. There is tremendous violence going on, killing for the sake of killing, for the fun of killing, violence not only with the gun but also violence that destroys people when they obey somebody. Please, this is a tremendous subject. Don't just take a part of it and say that I am against the army. We are dealing with the whole phenomenon of life, not just parts of it as the scientists, the doctors, the priests, and the educators are doing. We are concerned with the entirety of human life. If you like to pick just parts of it, that is up to you. That is perfectly right. But we are concerned with the whole of life, not only one's own particular life, but also the life of human beings throughout the world. There is immense, incalculable poverty that you don't know about, the indignity, the corruption of it. And there are all the religious circuses—sorry to use that word—all the religious nonsense that is going on in the world; it is a big business with Rolls Royces and tremendous activity.

We are concerned with the whole of humanity. We are also humanity—it is not that humanity is *there*, and we are different; we *are* humanity. We are not British, French, Russian; we are human beings first, nationals or professionals after. And we human beings have separated ourselves and that is why there is chaos in the world. Some may say, 'It is just a war in Lebanon, or the Far East, Afghanistan, or wherever, who cares!' But you feel deeply that you are the entire humanity because you suffer as they suffer, you shed tears as they do. You are anxious, you laugh, you have pain, and they too have all this, whether they are rich or poor. They are corrupt and so are we in a different way. They are corrupt because they want money, food, and they will do anything to have money and food, anything.

So we are the entire humanity. If you realize that marvellous thing, which is the truth, then you will not kill another, then there is no division between this country and that country, then your whole life is different. If you want to pick parts of it, go ahead. Nobody is putting pressure on you not to pick a part of it to satisfy your little demands, or your big demands. But if one actually, deeply, honestly, without all the ideological nonsense, sees the real fact that we are the whole of humanity—non-believers, Muslims, Hindus, Buddhists, the Christians—we are one. We all go through tremendous travail. Therefore, this search for individual freedom, individual becoming, and so on, becomes rather childish.

Sources and Acknowledgments

From the report of the sixth public talk in Poona, 3 October 1948, in volume V of *The Collected Works of J. Krishnamurti*, © 1991 Krishnamurti Foundation of America.

From the report of the second public talk at Rajghat, 23 January 1949, in volume V of *The Collected Works of J. Krishnamurti*, © 1991 Krishnamurti Foundation of America.

From the report of the first public talk in Rajahmundry, 20 November 1949 in volume VI of *The Collected Works of J. Krishnamurti*, © 1991 Krishnamurti Foundation of America.

From the report of the fifth public talk in Bombay, 12 March 1950, in volume VI of *The Collected Works of J. Krishnamurti*, © 1991 Krishnamurti Foundation of America.

From the report of the fifth public talk in London, 23 April 1952, in volume VI of *The Collected Works of J. Krishnamurti*, © 1991 Krishnamurti Foundation of America.

From the report of the nineteenth talk with boys and girls at Rajghat School, 31 December 1952, in volume VII of *The Collected Works of J. Krishnamurti*, © 1991 Krishnamurti Foundation of America.

From the report of the first public talk in Bombay, 8 February 1953, in volume VII of *The Collected Works of J. Krishnamurti*, © 1991 Krishnamurti Foundation of America.

From the report of the second public talk in Poona, 10 September 1958, in volume XI of *The Collected Works of J. Krishnamurti*, © 1991 Krishnamurti Foundation of America.

From a conversation with David Bohm at Brockwood Park, 18 May 1975, chapter 1 of *Truth and Actuality*, © 1977 Krishnamurti Foundation Trust, Ltd.

144 On Truth

From the recording of the third public dialogue at Saanen, 1 August 1975, © 1975/1995 Krishnamurti Foundation Trust, Ltd.

From the seventh public talk at Saanen, 25 July 1976, chapter 10 of *Truth and Actuality,* © 1977 Krishnamurti Foundation Trust, Ltd.

From the recording of a conversation with Buddhist scholars and Brockwood staff members at Brockwood Park, 28 June 1979, © 1979/1995 Krishnamurti Foundation Trust, Ltd.

From the recording of the second public question-and-answer meeting at Ojai, California, 8 May 1980, © 1980/1995 Krishnamurti Foundation Trust, Ltd.

From the recording of the second public talk in Bombay, 3 February 1985, © 1985/1995 Krishnamurti F6undation Trust, Ltd.

From the recording of the second public question-and-answer meeting in Bombay, 7 February 1985, © 1985/1995 Krishnamurti Foundation Trust, Ltd.

From the recording of the third public talk in Bombay, 9 February 1985, © 1985/1995 Krishnamurti Foundation Trust, Ltd.

From the fifth public talk at Saanen, 21 July 1985, chapter 5 of *Last Talks at Saanen 1985,* © 1986 Krishnamurti Foundation Trust, Ltd.

From the third public question-and-answer meeting at Saanen, 25 July 1985, chapter 8 of *Last Talks at Saanen 1985,* © 1986 Krishnamurti Foundation Trust, Ltd.

From the recording of the second public question-and-answer meeting at Brockwood Park, 29 August 1985, © 1985/1995 Krishnamurti Foundation Trust, Ltd.